Cuba's Foreign Policy
in the Middle East

Cuba's Foreign Policy in the Middle East

Damián J. Fernández

Westview Press
BOULDER & LONDON

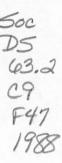

Westview Special Studies on Latin America and the Caribbean

This Westview softcover edition is printed on acid-free paper and bound in softcovers that carry the highest rating of the National Association of State Textbook Administrators, in consultation with the Association of American Publishers and the Book Manufacturers' Institute.

Published in 1988 in the United States of America by Westview Press, Inc.; Frederick A. Praeger, Publisher; 5500 Central Avenue, Boulder, Colorado 80301

Library of Congress Cataloging-in-Publication Data
Fernandez, Damian.
    Cuba's foreign policy in the Middle East/Damian J. Fernandez.
      p. cm.—(Westview special studies on Latin America and the
Caribbean)
    Bibliography: p.
    Includes index.
    ISBN 0-8133-7379-4
    1. Middle East—Foreign relations—Cuba. 2. Cuba—Foreign
relations—Middle East. 3. Cuba—Foreign relations—1959–   .
I. Title. II. Series.
DS63.2C9F47 1988
327.7291056—dc19   87-12509
                                                                                            CIP

Printed and bound in the United States of America

  The paper used in this publication meets the requirements of the American National Standard for
    Permanence of Paper for Printed Library Materials Z39.48-1984.

6   5   4   3   2   1

Contents

List of Tables..ix
Acknowledgments...xi

Introduction...1

CHAPTER 1
CUBAN FOREIGN POLICY FROM 1959 TO 1985:
AN OVERVIEW...7

Cuba's Foreign Relations in Perspective...8
The Initial Period: 1959-1967...8
Increasing Internationalism: 1968-1974..10
Active Internationalism: 1975-1980..11
Restrained Internationalism:
    1980 to the mid-1980s...14
The New Internationalism...15
Ideology and Foreign Policy...16
The Soviet Connection and Cuban Foreign Policy:
    Independence, Dependence, or Convergence?.......................17
The Cuban Foreign Policy Model...19
Bases of Cuban Foreign Policy...19
The Attraction of Cuba for the Third World................................23
Decision-Making in Cuban Foreign Policy.....................................24
The Costs of and Restraints on Cuban Foreign Policy............26
The Means of Cuban Foreign Policy..26
Conclusion...29
Notes...30

CHAPTER 2
CUBAN FOREIGN POLICY IN THE MIDDLE EAST:
1959-1987..35

Introduction..35
Cuba in the Middle East:
  Historical Background...36
An Overview of the Development of Cuba's
  Foreign Policy in the Middle East..37
Stages of Cuba's Policy in the Region...42
Cuban-Soviet Objectives and
  Policy Tenets in the Middle East...48
Cuba's Entrance into the Middle East:
  The Region, Soviet Perspectives in 1973,
  and the Attraction of Cuban Foreign Policy....................................50
The Arab View of Cuba..53
Implementation of Cuban Foreign Policy in the Middle East.....55
Cuba-Middle East Trade...57
Conclusion..61
Notes..61

CHAPTER 3
THE IMPLEMENTATION OF CUBAN FOREIGN POLICY
IN THE MIDDLE EAST: COUNTRY BY COUNTRY.................65

People's Democratic Republic of Yemen (PDRY or South
Yemen)..65
The Palestine Liberation Organization (PLO)...............................70
Syrian Arab Republic...75
Algeria...79
Iraq...82
Iran...85
Relations with Other Countries...88
Conclusion..94
Notes..94

CHAPTER 4
CUBAN-LIBYAN RELATIONS: A CASE STUDY.......................99

Objectives of Cuban and Libyan Foreign Policy.........................100
History of Diplomatic Relations...101
Nature and Scope of Bilateral Relations...107
Linkages..110

Prospects for Cuban-Libyan Relations and Implications for the U.S., Latin America, and the Middle East................111
Notes................112

CHAPTER 5
CUBAN FOREIGN POLICY IN THE MIDDLE EAST:
CONCLUSIONS................115

Risks, Options, Constraints................117
Cuban-Soviet Interaction................120
Domestic Benefits and Costs................122
Cuban Foreign Policy in the Middle East: Implications and Prospects................124
Notes................127

Appendix A................129
Appendix B: Bibliographic Note................133
Appendix C: An Overview of Middle Eastern Countries................135
Selected Bibliography................145
Index................153

Tables

2.1 An Overview of Cuba's Relations with Middle Eastern Countries and Groups (1985)..56

2.2 Cuba's Exports to Selected Middle Eastern Countries (1958-1985)..59

2.3 Cuba's Imports to Selected Middle Eastern Countries (1958-1985)..60

Acknowledgments

Several individuals and institutions have contributed to make this book possible. My professors at the Graduate School of International Studies, University of Miami, sparked my interest in this topic and commented on an earlier version of the manuscript. Professors Jaime Suchlicki and Enrique Baloyra deserve special recognition. Graciella Cruz-Taura and Humberto Leon of the Cuban Information System at G.S.I.S. helped me locate invaluable research sources. Jane Marchi, managing editor of the *Journal of Interamerican Studies and World Affairs*, was an insightful critic, a constant supporter, and a kind editor. Georgina Olano was much more than a first-rate typist, a good friend. Olga Nazario offered me much food for thought. Peter Hudson, an able research assistant, worked hard on gathering the information for Appendix C. The staff of the Hispanic Division of the Library of Congress were quite helpful, directing me to Cuban sources. Colorado College, through the Faculty Research and Development Program, facilitated the completion of this manuscript. Finally, to my family, my friends (that's you Marta), and to M., thank you.

Damián J. Fernández

Introduction

In spite of growing academic interest in the international relations of revolutionary Cuba, its foreign policy toward the Middle East has been a neglected field of scholarly interest. This is surprising given the quality as well as the quantity of contacts between the island and the Middle Eastern region. In fact, one could say that Cuba's activities in the region are the best kept secret of Cuban foreign policy. Fidel Castro's regime initiated contact with the area as early as the 1960s. In 1964-5 Ernesto ("Che") Guevara led a mission to assist the forces of Algerian independence. Since then, most of the attention devoted to Cuban foreign policy has tended to focus on dramatic events, such as the intervention in Angola and Ethiopia. The study of Cuba's foreign policy in the Middle East is important because it reflects both those tenets that have come to be recognized as typical of the island's international relations along with new dimensions introduced by the complex nature of, and situation in, the region itself.

Cuban foreign policy in the Middle East is based upon a position of support for the radical Arab states or groups who are opposed to Israel and the United States. Its objective is twofold: to further Soviet interests on the one hand, and to cultivate Cuba's national interest on the other. In pursuit of this objective, Cuba has followed the Soviet line in the Middle East and has developed its closest relations with regimes who are sympathetic to the Soviet Union. The fact that Cuba toes the Soviet line, however, should not be taken to mean that Cuba's only role in the area is that of proxy. Three theories are often put forth to explain, or categorize, the Cuban-Soviet relationship, i.e., that it is one of dependence; of independence (or autonomy); or of convergence of interests. Cuba's policy in the Middle East reveals a combination of all three, depending

1

on a set of variables previously neglected in other studies (see Appendix A).

Havana has publicly acknowledged that security is the paramount Soviet concern in the Middle East, and has willingly, so far as we know, integrated its policy there with that of Moscow. One way to reduce the inequality of the Soviet-Cuban partnership is to make Cuban foreign policy useful to the Soviet Union so that the U.S.S.R. needs Cuba to some extent; in place of total dependency, Castro seeks to introduce an element of interdependency. Through the medium of foreign policy, Fidel Castro and the revolutionary government can (a) gain leverage vis-a-vis the Soviet Union; (b) promote the cause of Cuban nationalism; (c) internationalize the Castro leadership; (d) acquire its own spheres of interest abroad; and (e) export national energy that could be problematic if it builds up domestically, especially in terms of export of surplus labor. Thus the motivation behind Cuba's insertion into the Middle East is comprised of three parts: dependence upon, a convergence of interests with, and an attempt to acquire and retain independence from the Soviet Union. Consequently, this study contends that, while the impetus for Cuba's Mid-East policy comes from ideology (i.e., Castroism and proletarian internationalism), the force that maintains it is pragmatism.

In addition, this study intends to demonstrate several hypotheses. First, Cuba's foreign policy in the Middle East is qualitatively and procedurally different from revolutionary foreign policy in other areas of the world. Second, Havana's approach to the region reflects ideological flexibility and pragmatism; nevertheless, the policy has remained faithful to the principles of Castroism. Third, Cuba has placed itself in a position of influence among Arab groups and countries. Therefore, Cuba is an important backstage actor in regional politics. Fourth, the Revolution's conduct of international relations during the past decade has increasingly turned from low level diplomacy to power politics. Fifth, Cuba's involvement in Middle Eastern politics has brought, and will continue to bring, certain benefits to the island. However, in spite of these rewards, there are risks and costs involved, among which is the possibility that confronted with factionalism among their Arab allies, those in charge of making and implementing Cuban foreign policy will side with different groups, awakening differences, otherwise dormant within the Cuban foreign policy apparatus. In short, factionalism abroad may translate into factionalism at home.

GENERAL BACKGROUND

Cuba's policies, and behavior, in the Middle East have undergone five phases: (1) the initial stage, which lasted from 1959 to 1973, was characterized by a certain ambivalence, in which Cuba gave its largely rhetorical support to militant Arab states at the same time that it maintained diplomatic relations with Israel; (2) a second stage, from 1973 to 1977, began with Cuba breaking diplomatic relations with Israel, in response to the OPEC (Organization of Petroleum Exporting Countries) initiative, the Arab-Israeli war, and Castro's own interest in the area. The culmination of this stage was the deployment of Cuban troops in Ethiopia; (3) the third stage began in 1977 and continued to 1985, a period which witnessed a diversification of Cuban activity into the areas of socio-economic cooperation and the difficult arena of diplomatic mediation; (4) a fourth stage, from 1981 to 1985, was characterized by cautious involvement and restrained activism; and, (5) a fifth stage, from 1986 to the present (1987), which reflects a new vigor in Cuba's relations with countries in the region.

As leader of the Non-Aligned Movement (NAM), and riding high on his post-Angola popularity, Castro extended the horizons of Cuban influence by assuming an active role in Mid-East politics. However, disappointments intervened. Among these were Cuba's relinquishing of the chairmanship of the Non-Aligned Movement (1981) and the failure to secure a coveted seat on the Security Council of the United Nations (1980), two events which served to signal a decline in Cuban prestige and power abroad. In the Middle East itself, Cuba suffered further setbacks to its influence when it failed to mediate successfully in the Iranian-Iraqi war. Nor was it any more effective in resolving the infighting among competing factions of the PLO and promoting unity. From 1981 to the mid-1980s, Cuba was forced to moderate its course in the Middle East and pursue a more cautious policy. Since 1986, there are signs of a new vigor in Cuba's activities in the Middle East.

Cuba's involvement in the Mid-East has produced important repercussions at every political level. At the local state level, Cuba now has access to Middle East government leaders of the highest rank and to government agencies and organizations. At the regional level, Cuban assistance, through various kinds of training, both civil and military, has served to strengthen the more militant of the anti-Israeli forces in the region. Internationally, in the larger realm of big power politics, Cuba's role and actions have resulted in furthering the influence and the interests of the Soviet Union. The U.S.S.R. has been able to exert its influence indirectly, thereby reducing risks to itself and its prestige while maintaining and keeping its options open. In an area of the world where the East-West confrontation lurks just offstage, Cuban penetration has served to undermine the interests of both Israel and the United States. Moreover, the possibility of an international terrorist connection has added another destabilizing element to an already complex situation.

Havana's closest friends in the region at large include Ethiopia, Algeria, the Polisario Front, the Palestine Liberation Organization (PLO), Syria, South Yemen, Iran, Iraq, Libya, and the Lebanese Communist Party. Not friends, but at least acquaintances, are Egypt, Kuwait, North Yemen, and Jordan. The radical Arab states look upon Cuba as a good source of trainers and advisers in the military and technical (development project) fields, including the special area of servicing advanced Soviet equipment. The opportunity to cooperate with Cuba reduces the need to depend upon the Soviet Union for this kind of assistance. Cuba has also lobbied effectively for the Arab cause in the United Nations, as well as within the Non-Aligned Movement; and Cuba has served as broker between the PLO and various groups in both Latin America and other parts of the Third World, whose support the PLO was seeking. Cuba is well placed to function as a go-between for Arab groups and their counterparts in the Western Hemisphere.

OUTLINE

To understand the guiding principles of, and thinking behind, Cuba's Mid-East policy, this study will begin by examining the island's international affairs as they have evolved from 1959 to the present, analyzing the various shifts that took place in foreign policy from the standpoint of the external-internal pressures being exerted. Chapter 1 offers an overview of Cuba's foreign policy since 1959. Thereafter, attention will focus upon the region itself. Chapter 2 intertwines two main topics (a) a brief analysis of the situation that existed in the Middle East at the time that Castro entered actively upon the scene in 1973; and (b) the means, ends, extent of, and reasons for Cuba's involvement in this area. Chapter 3 presents a close-up look of precisely how Cuba operates through a case-study approach which examines Cuban relations with several Arab countries. Chapter 4 focuses on Cuban-Libyan relations in some detail. Chapter 5 considers the effects which Cuba's Middle East policy has on the island, the local states, and the region, as well as on Cuba's relations with other countries. Additionally, the following questions will be addressed:

- What will be Cuba's probable policies in the future, given the current situation and trends?
- What are the regime's options and constraints?
- What risks does Cuba face?
- What are the implications of Cuba's actions for other players in the region, including the Arab countries, Israel, the United States, and the Soviet Union?
- What repercussions, if any, may Cuban Mid-East involvement have for stability-instability in the region? in the rest of the world?

SOME INITIAL OBSERVATIONS

The first question one must pose when embarking on the study of relations between countries is that of perspective. From what point of view will the analyst approach the topic? This is essential, for foreign policy brings together at least two agents, both of whom have their own agendas at heart and their own political processes which determine behavior. The present study is written from the perspective Cuban foreign policy. Conditions and events in the Arab countries and in the Middle East have been taken into account for foreign policy does not occur in a vacuum. Therefore, wherever appropriate, and within the limitations of the researcher, the Arab side is discussed, but in every case in function of what it has meant for Cuba's involvement in that region of the world. (For this purpose Appendix C offers brief sketches of the political and socio-economic conditions of the Arab countries with which Cuba has established relations.)

The second question that arises when one engages in such a study is how to define the region geographically. This study has been selective in its approach to the area by not including all the countries usually defined as Middle Eastern. I have focused on the countries with which Cuba has considerable contact. I have not included the Polisario Front or Ethiopia in the study, although from the Cuban foreign ministry perspective, they are part of the same area. The reasons for the omission are several. First, the Polisario Front and Eritrea involve a set of complex issues requiring separate discussion. Second, the interest of this writer centers on the countries that are intimately involved in confrontation with Israel.

Finally, given the type of primary data used in this study (government pronouncements, state-controlled radio broadcasts, and newspaper articles), the approach to the subject matter is that of "speculative analysis."[1] The closed nature of Cuba's political system poses analytical difficulties for the researcher.[2] Lack of data on how and why policy is made at times forces the

6

researcher to speculate on the significance of policy and to
assume a critical stance, all within a general historical
framework of the Cuban Revolution.

NOTES

1. Edward Gonzalez coined the term "speculative analysis."
Other scholars such as Andres Suarez have employed it to
describe the approach that they, as Cubanologists, take.

2. See "Bibliographic Note" (Appendix B).

1

Cuban Foreign Policy
from 1959 to 1985: An Overview

Fidel Castro first began to display an interest in the Middle East early in the 1960s. With the passage of time, this interest developed into a full-blown policy characterized by shifts in allegiance and a high degree of activism. Cuba's incursion into the Arab world provides an excellent example as to just how its foreign policy works, especially in relation to the recurring elements of autonomy, convergence, subordination vis-a-vis the Soviet Union, pragmatism, and ideology. Policy toward the Middle East reflects the changes that took place in Cuban foreign policy generally after 1959, including those of the 1980s following the Cuban experience in Angola, Ethiopia, and Grenada. On the whole, Castro's involvement with the Middle East poses significant risks to, and raises new challenges for, his regime.

Cuba has responded to these challenges by adopting new strategies in the pursuit of its goals, enabling it to adhere to traditional patterns in its international behavior. The result has been an approach to the region both flexible and pragmatic, yet always consistent with revolutionary ideology. The logic behind this foreign policy style has been one of reducing the risk of policy failure while maximizing Cuba's room to maneuver.

The following discussion will explore why, when, and how Cuba entered the area of the Middle East. This chapter will provide an overview of Cuban foreign policy, from several perspectives. First, it will survey, chronologically, the stages through which Cuban foreign policy has passed since 1959. Second, it will review the principal theories which have been applied to the analysis of Cuba's foreign relations. Third, it will discuss the influence which Soviet-Cuban relations have on Cuba's international activities. Fourth, it will examine the decision-making process by which Cuban foreign policy is

7

formulated. Finally, we will take a look at both the means and the ends of these policies. Combined, these perspectives should help us to understand Cuban actions and intentions in the convoluted politics of the Middle East.

CUBA'S FOREIGN RELATIONS IN PERSPECTIVE

From 1959 to the present, Cuba's foreign policy can be divided into four stages: (1) the initial period (1959-1967); (2) the period of increasing internationalism (1968-1974); and (3) the period of active internationalism (1975-1980).[1] To these categories should be added a fourth (and current) period which covers developments in the 1980s, under the rubric of limited or restrained internationalism (1981 to the mid-1980s).[2] Although it is still too soon to tell, the latter half of the 1980s may herald yet another stage in the island's international relations, one which may turn out to be called "the new internationalism."

THE INITIAL PERIOD: 1959-1967

During the first -- or initial -- stage, the main priority of the Cuban government was to stabilize, and consolidate, its Revolution. However, at the same time the seeds of its future internationalism were being sown. From 1959 to 1967, "Cuba's foreign policy can be viewed as exhibiting a restrained activism, restrained in the sense that many Cuban policy initiatives were responses and reactions to international conditions and were made necessary by the policies of other actors."[3] During this period, Cuba had neither the power -- nor the means -- to carry out extensive foreign activities, although the revolutionary elite had already begun to manifest its commitment to a globalist policy, especially in its support of revolutionary groups in Latin America.

While the antagonism of the United States served to circumscribe Cuba's foreign activities to some extent, Cuba did not respond passively -- or in merely reactive fashion -- to this posture. Since early in 1959, Castro consistently made decisions which served to foreclose U.S. economic assistance to, and trade with, the island.[4] Moreover, Castro's anti-Americanism, a cornerstone of his ideology, antedated 1959. The U.S. embargo, the termination of diplomatic relations, and the expulsion of Cuba from the Organization of American States (OAS) isolated Cuba within the Western Hemisphere. Castro's *guerrillismo* alienated Cuba in official circles throughout Latin America as

Havana preached revolutionary overthrow in other countries as well, and Ernesto ("Che") Guevara, one of Castro's revolutionary leaders, called for "many Vietnams." In practice, Cuba supported guerrilla movements at work in Argentina, Bolivia, Brazil, Chile, Colombia, Guatemala, Mexico, Nicaragua, Peru, Uruguay, and Venezuela. For this reason, this period has also been labeled the period of the export of revolution. Throughout Central and South America, guerrilla leaders, inspired by Castro, adopted the rural *foco* strategy to achieve power through armed uprisings which were designed to start in the countryside and spread to the urban areas (the model used by Castro). In this concept of revolution, Communist parties assumed a secondary role, if they were to participate at all. Unlike traditional Marxism-Leninism, Fidel's strategy does not assign a vanguard role to the Party.[5]

As Havana's relations with Washington rapidly deteriorated onto a confrontation course, Castro sought out the economic and moral support of Moscow. From the Castro perspective, only the Soviet Union had the power to ensure the survival of his Revolution from reprisal by the United States. Thereafter, the Soviet Union became the focus of Cuba's international relations despite the fact that Soviet-Cuban relations were often to suffer from their ups and downs. Cole Blasier claims that, although Castro's collision with the U.S. has received the most public scrutiny, actually Cuba's biggest battles were with its Soviet patrons throughout the 1960s.[6] Diverging interpretations of revolutionary strategy were not the only impediments to the Soviet-Cuban alliance.

The Soviets had their doubts about Castro's reliability as an ally: not only was Cuba involved in the Non-Aligned Movement (NAM) but it had also courted the friendship of the Chinese in the early-to-mid-1960s. The Cubans had their doubts as well, particularly regarding the degree of Soviet commitment to defend the Revolution. This was dramatized by the Kennedy-Khruschev negotiations at the time of the 1962 Missile Crisis, from which Castro was excluded, a situation which caused Castro to question the reliability of Soviet friendship. Tensions between Havana and Moscow continued to escalate up til 1968, when Castro resolved the conflict by agreeing (1) to endorse the Czechoslovakian invasion and (2) to abandon guerrillismo in Latin America.

Cuban involvement in Africa dates back to this initial period. In 1966 Havana hosted the First Conference of Solidarity with the Peoples of Africa, Asia, and Latin America, with the purpose of coordinating a common strategy to fight imperialism. Even before this date, Cuba had sent limited military aid to certain countries (such as Algeria and the Congo) in support of anti-colonial groups. Also in the 1960s, Che

Guevara had toured Africa to establish contacts and to offer assistance.[7]

During this stage, major foreign policy successes of the regime were the survival of the Revolution and defeat of the U.S.-sponsored invasion at the Bay of Pigs. The combination of fending off U.S. hostility and securing Soviet assistance provided Cuba with an international coup. Jorge Dominguez analyzed "the management of success" in Cuban foreign policy to conclude that:

> Above all, the Cuban revolutionary government wanted to survive after January 1959. For many regimes of the world, that might not necessarily be such an obvious foreign policy need, but it was by no means a foregone conclusion that the Cuban revolutionary regime would survive at any time between 1959 and 1962 ... The need for success was most pressing in the early years.[8]

INCREASING INTERNATIONALISM: 1968-1974

Cuba's foreign policy entered its second stage in 1968, when the Soviets were able to pressure Cuba, successfully, to support the Moscow line regarding the appropriate road to revolution in Latin America, and when Castro agreed, albeit reluctantly, to endorse the Soviet invasion of Czechoslovakia. After 1968, idealism became tempered by pragmatism. The pressures on Castro were not only external. Within the country the economy had been steadily deteriorating, and failure to reach Fidel's much-publicized projected 10-million-ton sugar harvest (in 1970) only underscored Cuba's need for Soviet economic assistance. In return for the latter, an "understanding" was reached with the Soviets regarding international policies, and Cuba's identification with the Soviets increased. As a result, Cuba accommodated to Soviet demands concerning its internal politics. By the early 1970s, Cuba had become integrated into the COMECON and had strengthened the Cuban Communist Party.

With military and economic aid guaranteed, the regime received the protection it needed to initiate global activism. In 1972 Castro travelled throughout Africa and Eastern Europe; in 1973 he gave a landmark speech in Algiers at the Non-Aligned Meeting. In this address, Castro condemned the notion of two imperialisms (that of the U.S. and the U.S.S.R.), and he defended the thesis that the Soviet Union, as a socialist and, therefore, an anti-imperialist state was a natural ally of the Third World in the struggle for freedom and development.

It was during this period that Cuba increased its military missions to Africa and the Middle East, as well as the number of foreign socio-economic assistance projects. By 1973, Cuban personnel were operating in Algeria, Angola, Equatorial Guinea, Iraq, Mozambique, Sierra Leone, Somalia, South Yemen, and Syria.[9] In Latin America, Castro opted for conventional state-to-state relations, having abandoned, at least temporarily, the incitement to revolution. The island found diplomatic doors opening as several Latin American countries (Peru, Panama, Colombia, Venezuela, and Chile under Allende) reestablished relations with Havana.

At the same time, Cuba and the U.S.S.R. decided that cooperation in the international arena could be mutually beneficial. Havana was assured of much needed Soviet economic and military assistance as relations intensified between the two regimes. Furthermore, Fidel's personal dream of becoming a revolutionary figure of world stature was given added substance as Cuba was able to diversify its contacts about the globe. This development was also encouraging to a domestic nationalism which would have liked to reduce dependency on the Soviets.

In turn, the Soviets were compensated for assuming the financial burden of supporting, and the risks incumbent in having, an unpredictable ally, by the benefits produced through a lowered international visibility which reduced their risk of confrontation with other powers as well as the cost of potential failures. As the Angolan, Ethiopian, and Grenadian situations were to demonstrate, years later, Cuba could serve as a broker for Soviet influence and a proxy for the Soviet presence.[10]

ACTIVE INTERNATIONALISM:
1975-1980

As the Soviet-Cuban connection grew stronger, the conditions Cuba needed to assume a more active international role were being met and the way paved to the third stage. In this sense, the 1968-1974 period served as a prelude for orchestration of the partners' diplomatic and military moves in several areas of the Third World. In 1975, three events took place which marked a new era in Cuban foreign relations: (1) the First Congress of the Communist Party of Cuba was held; (2) OAS sanctions against Cuba came to an end; and, (3) Cuban involvement in Angola escalated. As John McShane has pointed out, "the First Party Congress represented not the depersonalization of governance under Fidel, but rather a heightened concentration of power and responsibility on the líder máximo with respect to foreign policy."[11] Centralization of decision-making is illustrated by the fact that Fidel holds the first position in the Party, the Council of State, the Council of Ministers, and the Ministry of the Revolutionary Armed Forces (MINFAR).

With firm internal control, strong Soviet support, and the beginning of acceptance in the Hemisphere, and with Castroism as the driving force, Fidel Castro embarked on a period of unprecedented foreign activism. The reinvigorated international role found expression in traditional state-to-state diplomacy, a leadership role in the Third World movement, and in troop commitments abroad, specifically in Angola and Ethiopia. Cuba not only found new and old friends in the Caribbean (Panama, Mexico, Jamaica, Guyana, Trinidad-Tobago, and later Grenada), but also cultivated allies in the Middle East, Africa, and Europe. In 1977, Fidel made a successful tour of those continents. Two years later, in 1979, Cuba, as leader of the Non-Aligned Movement, acted as host for the Sixth Conference of Non-Aligned Nations, held in Havana.

The overthrow of Salvador Allende in Chile (1973), who had been the first socialist in Latin America to be elected head of state, had a profound impact on the Cuban-Soviet alliance. Both Havana and Moscow interpreted Allende's fall in the same way: by claiming that it was impossible for a progressive group to reach power by means of the ballot. Castro's line of the 1960s, that violence was the correct strategy to follow in the "liberation" of the Third World, appeared to be vindicated by the Chilean case. As a result, Soviet and Cuban views on revolution began to converge, eventually to be justified by the successful revolution in Nicaragua (1979). This ideological concert between Cuba and the Soviet Union made possible their future collaboration on military campaigns and brought the two countries closer together.

The best-known of these collaborative efforts are Cuba's missions to Angola and Ethiopia, both of which have been extensively documented.[12] Since 1975 Havana has sent Cuban soldiers (up to 36,000 according to Castro) to back the Marxist Popular Movement for the Liberation of Angola (MPLA) in its fight against opposition groups. In Angola, Cuba provided the manpower while the Soviets furnished the weapons and logistical infrastructure. It was a massive operation which decided the outcome in favor of the MPLA's Agostinho Neto. In spite of the apparent triumph, Cuba incurred considerable costs, not only financial and human, but also in terms of popular support, the extent of which have yet to be determined as the campaign continues.

In the Ethiopian-Somalian conflict, Cuba found itself in the embarassing position of supporting first one, then the other, side in this struggle. In 1974, Cuba had established a military mission in Somalia, at which time it had supported that country's territorial claim against Ethiopia. When, in 1975, there came to power in Ethiopia a radical, pro-Soviet faction, led by Lt. Col. Mengistu Haile Mariam, Cuba established relations with the new government. This sufficiently offended the Somalis that they retaliated by seeking support from the West. During a visit to the area in 1977, Castro attempted to mediate the conflict between Ethiopia and Somalia personally, but the effort failed and Somalia invaded the disputed region (the Ogaden) in July 1977. The following year, when the Ethiopian forces were on the verge of defeat in 1978, Cuban forces staged a counter-offensive. By April 1978, 15,000 Cuban soldiers were fighting in Ethiopia, using Soviet-provided weaponry and under Soviet command. Confronted by counterattack, the Somalis were forced to pull back, and the war was subsequently decided in favor of Ethiopia.[13]

Despite their cost, the African campaigns had positive repercussions for Cuba's international relations. As H. Michael Erisman has written: "In essence, then, the Angolan involvement transformed Cuba from a regional power with wider ambitions to a full-fledged player on the global stage."[14] Initially, the Third World and the African nations responded favorably to Cuban involvement. Increasingly, however, African governments began to equate Cuban objectives with those of the Soviets, a realization which served to undermine Havana's professions of non-alignment (especially after Cuban approval of the invasion of Afghanistan). Nevertheless, the African wars raised the prestige and power of revolutionary Cuba.[15] At the same time, the African wars increased Cuba's leverage vis-a-vis Moscow.

As Cuba's value to the Kremlin became more apparent, Soviet military and economic aid to the island climbed to unprecedented levels. A five-year economic agreement, signed in 1976, provided for a 250% increase in trade between the two countries as compared with the previous five-year period. The accord also provided for the building of a nuclear power plant and a steel mill, as well as for the indexing of the price of Soviet crude oil to the price of Cuban sugar.[16]

The Angolan and Ethiopian actions also carried internal political ramifications. First, changes in the state and Party organs enhanced the power of hard-line *fidelistas* at the expense of the pragmatists (the technocratic and managerial elite).[17] Second, and related to the above, the Revolutionary Armed Forces (*Fuerzas Armadas Revolucionarias*, FAR) gained prominence and clout. Pleased with the FAR's accomplishments, Moscow rewarded it with modern weaponry. For U.S.-Cuban relations, however, Havana's expanded activism proved detrimental. The thaw, which had begun under Ford and continued under Carter, ended abruptly when Washington asked Havana to withdraw its troops from Africa and Cuba refused.

RESTRAINED INTERNATIONALISM: 1980 TO THE MID-1980s

The fourth stage of Cuban foreign policy, that of restrained activism (or "partial paralysis"),[18] began in 1980. In 1979, when Cuba officially sanctioned the Soviet invasion of Afghanistan, it damaged its non-aligned credentials with the Third World. Cuba also followed the Soviet position on Kampuchea during the debate in the 1979 General Assembly, another position incompatible with non-alignment. As a result, the non-aligned nations failed to support Cuba's bid to become the non-permanent Latin American representative on the United Nations Security Council.

During this period, a few Latin American neighbors distanced themselves from Cuba when the Castro regime refused, on several occasions, to recognize the right of asylum.[19] The regime's isolation was made obvious when Mexico, responding to U.S. pressure, failed to invite Castro to the North-South Conference held in Cancun (in October 1981) to discuss the economic situation of the Third World and its relations to the industrialized countries. Cuba's absence underlined the extent to which its influence with the Third World had deteriorated.

Cuba's problems worsened with the inauguration of a Republican president in the White House. A staunch anti-communist, Ronald Reagan came to office determined to halt radical leftist regimes from proliferating in the U.S. backyard. Viewing national revolutions as part of the East-West conflict, the administration blamed Soviet-Cuban subversion for fomenting instability in Central America. To deal with this situation, the President adopted a hardline policy toward Cuba, including flexing military muscle in the Caribbean Basin, funding the *contras* in Nicaragua, supplying aid to fight the Salvadoran guerrillas, and eventually invading Grenada, a close ally of Havana.

Although Cuba scored a major foreign policy success when the Sandinistas overthrew Anastasio Somoza and took power in Nicaragua (in 1979), for the most part it had been losing friends in the region. A wave of neo-conservatism in the Caribbean washed away left-of-center governments in Jamaica, St. Vincent, St. Kitts-Nevis, Antigua, and St. Lucia. Cuban support for Argentina during the Falklands-Malvinas war improved relations between both countries, and, although Cuba had partially mended its fences with Venezuela, overall Havana's relations with its neighbors in the Americas were at a low point in the early 1980s. Relations with Colombia suffered due to Cuba's support for the M-19 guerrilla movement, and relations with Costa Rica suffered due to Cuba's treatment of political prisoners. Ties with Panama, Peru, and Ecuador weakened as democratic centrist regimes took office.

By the mid-1980s, Cuban foreign policy no longer reflected the activism of the preceding decade. Havana retreated to a wait-and-see posture and pursued conventional diplomacy. Certainly, the reversal in Grenada made the Cuban leadership aware of its limitations and affected Cuban international behavior. Following Grenada, Castro warned Nicaragua that Cuba would not be able to rescue the Sandinistas in the event of U.S. military invasion.[20]

Grenada provoked internal repercussions as well, specifically within the FAR. The invasion chilled Cuban-Soviet ties for approximately a year and a half due to what Havana considered Moscow's detachment from the Grenadian crisis. It seems that Castro, under attack from leftist groups in the region for "abandoning" his allies to U.S. imperialism, criticized Soviet lack of support for revolutions. Implicitly, he may have been drawing parallels between the Grenadian situation and his own under like circumstances, questioning Soviet resolve to come to the aid of its friends.[21]

After a series of foreign policy setbacks in the 1980s and an extended stay in Africa, Cuba began to re-emphasize traditional means of furthering its international aims. These included a renewed effort at establishing, or repairing, state-to-state relations and organizing regional conferences on topics of widespread interest (i.e., the debt crisis). Retreating from the activism suggested by military ventures, Havana is now returning to the political arena by courting domestic Latin American political actors, such as organized labor and religious groups. In a pragmatic vein, Cuba is developing connections with capitalist and oil-exporting countries which may one day prove to be sources for much-needed capital and markets. Vis-a-vis Washington, Castro continues to oscillate between overt antagonism and overtures for normalization, a see-saw pattern likely to endure for the foreseeable future.[22]

THE NEW INTERNATIONALISM

Superseding this restrained internationalism, there appears to be in the making a stage of "new internationalism," characterized by diplomatic initiatives on a variety of fronts (i.e., the debt crisis) and by an ideological flexibility which allows for the cultivation of newfound friends (i.e., liberation theology). This approach casts Fidel Castro in the role of elder statesman and attempts to place Cuba in the position of powerbroker, in a new initiative to recapture worldwide influence. The new internationalism does not repudiate Havana's commitment to revolutionary change and ideology, but it does seek to extend diplomatic influence abroad without high risk or costs for the island.

Given previous setbacks and the level of, and the problems associated with, Cuba's military involvement overseas, the revolutionary leadership seems unwilling, or unable, to pursue the policies of the mid-1970s. Therefore, statesmanship, moderation, and expansion of socio-economic ties have become salient features of the island's international behavior. This is not to say that such an approach was absent from Cuban foreign policy in the past. Not at all. In fact, it has always been present to some degree. The only change has been one of emphasis.

Both the revolutionary internationalism *a la* Angola and the restrained internationalism of the early 1980s have become unpalatable for the time being. In the Middle East, as well as in other regions of the world, the new internationalism is being put into practice. It is still too early to evaluate its outcome.

IDEOLOGY AND FOREIGN POLICY

Although Marxism, the official ideology of the regime, sets parameters on behavior if not on rhetoric, it is Castroism, as a set of fixed beliefs, that illuminates Havana's foreign policy best. The relationship between Marxism and Castroism has not been thoroughly studied. Marxism and Castroism share certain commonalities: for instance, an emphasis on revolution, centralization of state power, and anti-imperialism. Marxism dictates ideological expansionism; in practice, Castroism has also pursued this goal.

Andres Suarez has characterized Castroism as consisting of the following principles: (1) the assimilation of social change by revolutionary change; (2) revolutionary change requires as a necessary condition the monopoly of the state apparatus; (3) seizure of the state presupposes the application of violent means, initially as guerrilla war, later through creation of a politico-military organization commanded by a leader who exercises both political and military roles; (4) revolutionary victory demands popular mobilization; and, (5) mass mobilization is facilitated by sophisticated manipulation, especially the elaboration of some variety of anti-imperialist nationalism, preferably identified with a historical personality able to be mythologized.[23] This ideological framework helps explain Cuba's foreign policy.

Castroism permeates Cuba's internal and external politics. The Cuban domestic system has had widespread impact on the foreign policy-making process. Centralization of power in the lider maximo points to a lack of institutionalization in policymaking. State control of mass organization facilitates foreign policy initiatives by serving as transmission belts for state decisions.

THE SOVIET CONNECTION AND CUBAN FOREIGN POLICY: INDEPENDENCE, DEPENDENCE, OR CONVERGENCE?

The meaning of Cuban-Soviet relations for Havana's external pursuits have been analyzed from three different perspectives: independence (or autonomy), dependence or subordination (the satellite, proxy or surrogate thesis), or convergence (overlapping interests). The independence thesis claims that Cuban foreign policy stems primarily from the perceptions of national interest defined by the revolutionary elite. Cuba's actions are nationalistic, disregarding at times the wishes of the island's closest friend and benefactor, the Soviet Union. To substantiate their claims, the proponents of this view present instances of Soviet-Cuban conflicts over foreign affairs decisions.[24] Cuba's support of guerrillas in Latin America throughout the 1960s is but one example of this. According to the independence thesis, Cuba acts on the moral basis of proletarian internationalism. Internationalism results from the regime's solidarity with oppressed people, and with underdeveloped countries (or groups) who seek to liberate themselves from imperialism and underdevelopment by means of a socialist revolution. Logically, then, this appraisal sees Cuba as a non-aligned country.

The surrogate perspective takes a position contrary to that of the independence thesis. This view states that Cuba's international activities are dictated and conditioned by Soviet interests, the price Havana must pay for its economic and security dependence on Moscow. Similar to East European socialist countries, Cuba is a satellite of the Soviet Union and must act accordingly. As a consequence, the island's foreign policy is an instrument by which the Kremlin spreads its influence indirectly throughout the Third World. From this vantage point, Havana's international relations are not unaligned, but integrated with, and subordinated to, Soviet global objectives. Cuba's involvement in Africa is viewed solely as a war-by-proxy. In most academic circles, however, the total dependency thesis is considered simplistic.[25]

The convergence thesis holds that mutual interests make cooperation between Cuba and the U.S.S.R. both beneficial and natural. Both states espouse socialism, revolution, and anti-imperialism. While Cuba adds to its prestige as its power and influence branches out worldwide, it also increases its leverage vis-a-vis the Kremlin through active foreign initiatives. At the same time, the Soviet Union gains access to, and influence on, other countries through collaboration with the Cubans. This policy reduces risks to Moscow by concealing its involvement. Supporters of the convergence thesis, such as Jorge Dominguez and Edward Gonzalez, underscore the joint Cuban-Soviet venture in Angola and Ethiopia--the Cubans supplied soldiers, the Soviets supplied arms. Both countries gained from the involvement. As evidence of Cuban semi-independence, these observers claim that the decision to intervene in Angola was initiated by Cuba and backed by Moscow.

A more accurate analysis takes into account varying degrees of dependence and independence in a specific case. Edward Gonzalez, for instance, claims that Cuba, although self-motivated in its foreign policy, acts within Soviet parameters while pursuing its own interests. Jorge Dominguez recognizes the Soviets' dominant position relative to Cuba but concludes that the relationship has evolved into one of mutual dependency, giving Cuba its own space to formulate foreign policy. Other scholars (Jiri Valenta and David Ronfeldt) emphasize the existence of a special relationship between Moscow and Havana, due to such factors as distance and Castro's leadership.[26]

Rather than subscribing to any one of these three perspectives, it is preferable to look at Cuba's foreign policy on a case-by-case basis instead of endorsing any one thesis *a priori*. Depending on the region, country, and on the issue, Cuba's past initiatives have been both dependent on and, independent of, the Kremlin at various times. In Central and Latin America, due to proximity and cultural affinity, Cuba has more room to act than in the Middle East (See Appendix A for further theoretical discussion). In any case, Cuba has not pursued a course contrary to Soviet interests since the mid-1960s. The Soviet connection has entailed foreign policy constraints, self-imposed or not. In this regard, it is possible to argue that the Soviet influence has restrained Castro's activism. On the other hand, without Moscow's financial support, Cuban military and socio-economic missions abroad would be seriously handicapped, if feasible at all.

THE CUBAN FOREIGN POLICY MODEL

In the literature on the international behavior of small states, Cuba is usually set aside as an exception to the rule. Due to the limitations imposed on them by size and underdevelopment, small states generally limit their activities in the international arena. This type of state tends to be characterized by reliance on verbal (versus non-verbal) recourse, the pre-eminence of economic considerations in foreign relations, and employment of cost-effective mechanisms for foreign policy implementation.[27] Cuba's internationalism since 1959 does not conform to this pattern. Two main variables explain this: Castroism (and Castro himself) and the partnership with the Soviet Union (which facilitates the opportunities and the financial resources to play global power politics).

BASES OF CUBAN FOREIGN POLICY

Cuban foreign policy revolves around two poles: pragmatism and ideology. Depending on the issue and the context, the island's international behavior stresses one or the other. Ideology is evident in the official documents of the Cuban Communist Party (PCC). The Programmatic Platform adopted by the First Congress of the PCC in December 1975 stipulates that "Proletariat Internationalism constitutes the essence and the departure point of the international politics of the Cuban Communist Party."[28] According to the same document, the basis of the island's foreign policy is: "The subordination ... of Cuba's interests to the general interests of the struggle for socialism and communism, national liberation, the defeat of imperialism and the elimination of colonialism, neo-colonialism and all forms of exploitation and discrimination of nations and peoples."[29] A fundamental objective of foreign policy is to "supply, to the extent of our possibilities, economic cooperation and technological assistance to other underdeveloped countries of the world whose governments struggle sincerely to find adequate and fair solutions to socio-economic problems."[30]

The cornerstone of Cuba's internationalism is its close cooperation with the Soviet Union, in both practical and ideological terms. This is clearly expressed in the 1976 Constitution of the Republic of Cuba and the PCC platform. The Soviet Union is portrayed as the leader of the socialist movement and the struggle against U.S. imperialism. Cubans are repeatedly reminded that the U.S.S.R. is a close friend who came to the Revolution's rescue in its hour of need. In return, Castro has pledged that "We are and will continue always to be

friends of a generous people who have helped us so much ..."[31]
In spite of the ideological connection, the Soviet-Cuban
relationship, as Enrique Baloyra has written, is based mainly on
self-interest:

> To counteract U.S. hostility, Cuba did not renounce the
> friendship of the Soviet sphere, thus protecting itself
> from the economic embargo and lessening the economic
> pitfalls on the road to socialism. In dealing with the
> Soviet Union, Cuba--mainly in its self-interest--unfurled
> the banners of militant internationalist solidarity to
> maintain its own sphere of influence within the
> international system and in both cases to strengthen itself
> ideologically and diplomatically vis-a-vis the Soviet
> Union.[32]

Despite the practical benefits, this foreign policy outlook fits
well with Castroism's emphasis on anti-Americanism and
revolutionary activism. Marxism-Leninism is a vehicle to carry
out these goals:

> The Communist Party of Cuba considers itself a modest
> but reliable detachment of the international communist
> movement ... Our party participates in this program in
> an independent fashion but, at the same time, with
> complete loyalty to the common cause, joined with
> communists from other countries.[33]

Castroism and Marxism are change-oriented. Above all,
Castro considers himself a revolutionary. These factors have
implications for Cuba's international relations, especially when
coupled with ingrained anti-U.S. attitudes since Castro's initial
revolutionary pronouncements. A basic document to understand
the regime's foreign policy, according to Carlos Martinez
Salsamendi, principal adviser to the Vice-President of Cuban
Council of State, is the Second Declaration of Havana (February
1962). The Declaration claims that "The duty of every
revolutionary is to make revolution."[34]
Since 1979 Castro has toned down his international
revolutionary activism and even his rhetoric at key moments.
Speaking at the U.N. in October 1979, the Cuban Prime Minister
stressed that:

> I have not come here as the prophet of revolution ... I
> have come to speak about peace and cooperation between
> nations ... let us say goodbye to arms...

In the speech he proceeded to defend peaceful coexistence, but clarified that:

> By peaceful coexistence we want everyone to understand that contradiction [between socialism and capitalism] shall come through ideological opposition and political struggle . . .[35]

Castro's words of peace and restraint are in sharp contrast to his actions on behalf of the FSLN in Nicaragua at the same time. During the late 1970s, Cuba moved rapidly to assist the Sandinistas with guidance and material support to overthrow Anastasio Somoza. After 1979, the Cubans continued their commitment to the survival of the Sandinistas and also backed insurgent groups in El Salvador, albeit less successfully.

In sum, as defined by official Cuban sources, the principles that guide Cuba's foreign behavior are: proletarian internationalism and solidarity with peoples of the Third World in their struggle for national liberation. In this regard, Castro has stated that "The duty of all progressive countries is to give consequent and unconditional aid to those who are engaged in a war of national liberation or suffer imperialist aggression anywhere in the world."[36] While the regime has also conducted traditional diplomatic relations with non-communist countries, the affinities are greater with anti-western revolutionary states and groups. Logically, this bipolarity leads to, and has resulted in, tension in the conduct of foreign policy.

From the Cuban perspective, the U.S. is the source of all global ills. The U.S., a capitalist Goliath, is responsible for colonialism and neo-colonialism in the Third World, conditions which cause underdevelopment and exploitation. The financial crisis now threatening the world system is, according to Cuba, the result of U.S. economic policies. Washington has been the main obstacle to the creation of a new international economic order. In issues of war and peace, the U.S. is also to blame. In a world of inequality, peace is improbable. Furthermore, the risk of a nuclear holocaust results from the U.S.-inspired arms race.

Cuba's view of the U.S. has roots in history. In the 1980s, Castro has found it easy to emphasize the nefarious features of the U.S. system due to President Reagan's worldview. According to Cuba, Reagan's militarism, conservative economic policies, and renaissance of U.S. willingness to oppose revolutions abroad have been detrimental to the well-being of the South. Castro has used this argument to arouse anti-Americanism in the Third World. The most recent example is Havana's regional conference on the debt crisis.[37]

As empirical theory suggests, the foreign policy analyst should consider acts rather than words as the variables to explain the causes and consequences of one state's relationship with another. Official statements, nevertheless, provide insights into why actions are taken. Ideology serves as a useful background against which to understand behavior. With this in mind, it is not appropriate to reach conclusions on Cuban foreign policy solely on the basis of state documents. Basic goals derive from the configuration of foreign policy events. Following this logic, one would agree with Baloyra that the three tenets of Cuba's international relations, in practical terms, are: (1) rejection of any sort of relationship that might erode the legitimacy and coherence of the regime; (2) close collaboration with the Soviet Union while following an independent line; and, (3) promotion of militant internationalism in order to maintain a sphere of Cuban influence in the international system and the communist movement.[38]

First of all, Cuba's foreign policy seeks to strengthen the revolution and the leadership position of the *fidelista* elite. One of the ways this is accomplished is by exporting national energy, thereby diverting the population's attention away from domestic matters to international affairs. Foreign policy serves then to funnel discontent into other lands, diffusing immediate pressure on the government from domestic sources, such as elite factions and mass discontent.

This safety valve effect of foreign policy works in several ways. First, intra-elite factionalism, as between civilian and military elites, is played out in capital cities, other than Havana. For instance, embassy personnel in Aden in the late 1970s, led by Osmani Cienfuegos, supported a moderate faction within the South Yemeni ruling group, while the military mission supported the hard-line, Soviet-aligned faction. Second, this incident also reveals that Cuban foreign policy is dynamic and not monolithic, prone to bureaucratic politics. Although Fidel Castro is the main source of foreign policy, there is a diverse, active, and at times conflicting, secondary level of policy-making.

Foreign policy channels political problems of the regime in other ways as well. Individuals who fall from the government's good graces and could become a source of discomfort if they remain on the island are sent abroad. Similarly, an excess in the labor force is less of a political risk in a weak economy if it is exported to distant lands than if it were to remain at home. Once again, national energy is exported to diffuse potential internal malaise. However, failure in foreign policy can generate serious difficulties for the regime. (The decisions of the Argentinian military to invade the Malvinas is a case in point.)

International policies provide other benefits. First, they extend the influence--if not the power--of the lider maximo while at the same time serving both the national interest as well as that of the Soviets. Second, and inter-related with the first, the regime wins friends and cultivates clients and adds to its autonomy, not to mention its bargaining power with the Kremlin.

THE ATTRACTION OF CUBA
FOR THE THIRD WORLD

The activism and success of Cuban foreign policy is partly due to the receptiveness of other countries to Havana's overtures. The Cuban Revolution appeared heroic to many sympathizers around the world. Small Third World countries identified with the island and saw their own aspirations realized by a revolutionary group pledged to break chains of imperialism, dependency, and underdevelopment, ousting a dictator supported by Washington. Havana's international and domestic policies became models for countries in similar circumstances.

Although scholars question whether the Cuban model can be transferred successfully to other countries,[39] Cuba sets an example for the Third World in other ways. First, the island has been able to cut its dependence on a capitalist metropolitan power--the United States. The *dependencia* theory, espoused by official and academic circles throughout Latin America and the Third World, claims that underdevelopment is a result of the exploitative relationship between powerful capitalist countries and poor peripheral states. Detaching the national economy from the international capitalist system is presented as a way out of backwardness; socialism is presented as the road to equality and prosperity. Second, Castroism combines revolutionary socialism with nationalism, both of which appeal to ideological currents in Third World countries. Orthodox Marxism-Leninism, on the contrary, downplays nationalism. Therefore, Cuba offers a new socialist modality for nationalist revolutions elsewhere. Third, the fidelista regime has evolved an idealistic ethical code (i.e., the new man, the virtue of work, international solidarity) which, although mythical, is attractive. Fourth, the Cuban political system fuses centralized personal power with bureaucratic institutions of mass participation, offering, at the very least, a fasade of citizen input into decision-making. Fifth, in spite of its links with the Soviets, Cuba continues to defend the principle of non-alignment, a demonstration of independence which Third World countries admire.

For radical states, Cuba offers an alternative to direct Soviet presence. In this sense, Havana is less threatening than

Moscow. At the same time, relations with Havana allow Third World states to maintain their credentials as non-aligned states, while, at the same time, they are receiving military assistance and or economic aid. By diversifying their partners, governments feel less vulnerable to penetration by a single outside power. Moreover, the experience of Angola, Ethiopia, and other African states indicates that it is easier for Third World governments to communicate and deal with the Cubans than with the Soviets. An Angolan official observed that:

> When the Soviets arrive here, they usually demand rooms in the best hotels or well-furnished houses ... which costs us a lot of our precious foreign exchange--whereas we can put five or six Cubans in a hot one-bedroom apartment with mattresses on the floor and we will never hear a complaint.[40]

The racial background of a portion of the Cuban population and the colonial history of the island also facilitates mutual identification between Cuba and the Third World.

DECISION-MAKING
IN CUBAN FOREIGN POLICY

Decision-making in revolutionary Cuba has been characterized by centralization of power not on party and state institutions, but on Fidel Castro, himself. In spite of the 1970s attempt to develop institutions which would formalize the process of making policy, the ultimate authority in Cuba is still Fidel. He has the power to make decisions in any and all domestic and external issues, power which he exercizes.

Nevertheless, decision-making is not as monolithic as it might appear. In practice, it is a two-tiered process. One tier is comprised of Fidel, who holds the last word; whereas the second tier is composed of the other members of the elite and the technocrats. It is within this secondary level of policy-making that different options are developed. Bureaucratic actors and individuals support one option or another according to individual or institutional preferences. As in any other bureaucracy, factions are bound to arise.

Groups and individuals within the party and the state agencies defend those policy alternatives which best fulfill their goals (be they personal ambition or an ideologically based interpretation of the common good). Consequently, the FAR may prefer to expand Cuba's military commitment in a given country, but the Ministry of Foreign Relations may oppose that option. The two tiers interact when, based on information provided by those who present policy options, Fidel makes the final choice. Everyone bows to this final decision. As Juan Benemelis, a Cuban ex-official, asserts, in this way Fidel acts as the great synthesizer.[41]

After Fidel has laid out the course to be followed, there is still room for various other players to make a contribution at the implementation stage. For instance, in the early 1970s a decision was made to cultivate relations with South Yemen. Personnel of both the Foreign Ministry and the FAR established contacts and worked to establish friendly relations with their South Yemeni counterparts. However, since factionalism was rampant within the Yemeni government itself, in 1978 the Cubans found themselves in a dilemma as to which of the contending groups to support. The embassy staff (under the direction of Osmani Cienfuegos) sided with the most moderate group, and the FAR mission (directed by Carlos Rafael Rodriguez) with the more pro-Soviet.[42] This is an instance in which domestic Cuban factionalism was played out on a stage overseas. The final decision as to which group should be supported in Yemen was made by Castro--in favor of the pro-Soviet faction backed by the FAR and Rodriguez. Cienfuegos eventually lost his position as regional *charge d' affaires*, apparently replaced by Rodriguez, which reflected a closer alignment with Moscow.

State and party departments, the second tier of decision-making in Cuba, are nominally in charge of foreign policy. At the level of state bureaucracy, the Ministry of Foreign Relations is the largest body to deal with foreign policy. Within that Ministry, the Department for Africa and the Middle East is responsible for that whole area. Although Fidel appoints individual directors for sub-regions (who are not necessarily officials of the Ministry), from an organizational point of view, Africa and the Middle East are defined as one area. Africa takes precedence, in the eyes of the Ministry, due to Cuba's involvement in Angola and Ethiopia, Cuba's cultural affinity with Africa, and the island's long-standing contact with African countries (since the early 1960s).

At the Party level, foreign affairs come under the jurisdiction of the Department of Foreign Relations of the Central Committee. Within this Department there is an African section, which focuses on the Middle East as well. Up to the late 1970s, ambassadors to the area have been connected with the Central Committee.

The General Directorate of Investigation (*Dirección General de Investigación*, DGI), part of the internal security apparatus, is engaged in operations abroad. DGI members work in association with Cuban embassies or consulates. Their function is that of espionage and intelligence. The DGI is influenced, if not controlled, by the Soviet KGB, and it provides the Cuban and the Soviet elite with security information for decision-making.

Other state agencies, such as the Union of Caribbean Enterprises (*Unión Nacional de Empresas del Caribe,* UNECA) and the Ministry of Construction Abroad are involved in international relations through socio-economic transactions. These agencies, however, are policy instruments rather than policy initiators.

THE COSTS OF
AND RESTRAINTS ON
CUBAN FOREIGN POLICY

Economic and political costs, as well as any potential for failure, deter Cuban activism abroad. Although centralized, one-party systems do not have to respond to popular pressures as do electoral democracies, it is logical to assume that the political elite (or the lider maximo) calculates the cost-benefit ratio of each foreign involvement during the decision-making process. Up to the present, the regime has been willing and able to defray the cost of its international activities. Political and economic liabilities in Angola are identified and discussed in the next chapter. General costs of foreign policies pursued since 1975 are as follows:[43] (1) less flexibility to diversify foreign relations; (2) undermining of non-aligned credentials; (3) economic cost of resources committed abroad, which has translated into loss of profitable investment opportunities and decrease in domestic production; (4) divisions within the political elite as to wisdom of these costs; (5) unpopularity (reluctance against) of international solidarity due to the possibility of participating in military service abroad; and, (6) deterioration in U.S.-Cuban relations.

These negative repercussions may act as a check on the island's overseas activities. One school of thought claims that the Soviet Union restrains Castro's impulse to involve Cuba in revolutions outside its borders, thereby serving as a moderating force. However, the lider maximo's unpredictable style and his ideology is bound to temper such cost-benefit considerations.

THE MEANS OF
CUBAN FOREIGN POLICY

To achieve its foreign policy goals and objectives, the regime employs various tools depending on the issue, region, and context: state-to-state diplomacy, international organizations and forums, military assistance, socio-economic development aid, support to insurgent groups and radical factions, and propaganda and disinformation. Like most other states, the bulk of Cuba's diplomatic business has been conventional state-to-state dealings. In spite of the regime's radicalism, relations with established governments have taken precedence over subversion and support for the Left.[44] This has not excluded, of course, intimacy with revolutionary movements worldwide.

The coexistence of peaceful diplomacy with "illegal" intervention has been a hallmark of Cuban foreign policy. For Cuba, conforming to the rules of international diplomatic behavior is both a necessity, (for, in this respect, no country is an island unto itself), and a way to escape U.S.-sponsored isolation. Through recognition of Castro's government, establishment of ties, opening of embassies, and expansion of commercial relations, the international community conferred *de facto* legitimacy on the revolution and supplied it with an economic lifeline to the outside world. Diplomacy, even with conservative states such as Franco's Spain, contributed to the survival of the Revolution, the primary objective of Castro's foreign policy. The pattern of government-to-government relations inaugurated in 1959 has continued to the present, thus giving Cuba acceptance within the family of nations. Cuba's "great power" actions have accelerated this trend. Dominguez notes that "the language of Cuban diplomacy has changed along the way. While there is still attention to the ideological foundations of Cuban foreign policy, there is increasing use of the language of high diplomacy."[45]

Cuba has used international organizations as forums within which to expound the worldview of its regime and as means to cultivate prestige and influence. The only Latin American country to participate in the creation of the Non-Aligned Movement in 1961, the island has held high-ranking positions on the NAM coordinating committee. In the Group of 77, Cuba has been among the most vociferous proponents of the New International Economic Order (NIEO). In the United Nations, Cuba has played on the *tercermundista* current to lobby for a host of issues generally anti-U.S., and pro-Soviet, under the guise of anti-colonialism and anti-imperialism. This emphasis on internationalism has made Havana the setting for global and regional conferences coordinated either multilaterally (such as the Tricontinental Conference) or unilaterally (such as the July 1985 Conference on the Latin American foreign debt crisis).

Among the issues that Cuba has defended and espoused in international organizations or forums are: (1) the independence of Puerto Rico; (2) independence for other colonial territories; (3) support for Salvador Allende's government in Chile (1970-3); (4) the transfer of the Panama Canal to the Panamanians; (5)

Argentina's claim to the Falklands or Malvinas; (6)
condemnation of the U.S. invasion of Grenada; (7) Zionism as a
form of racism; (8) a Palestinian homeland; (9) the illegality of
U.S. actions against Nicaragua (i.e., support for the *contras* and
mining of the harbors); (10) the need for the NIEO; (11) nuclear
freeze and an end to the arms race; and, (12) a negotiated
solution to the crisis in El Salvador (power-sharing).[46] Cuba's
influence in the Non-Aligned Movement is witnessd by the
frequency with which these topics are included in the
movement's final reports and on its agenda.

Foreign aid is another tool of Cuban foreign policy. As
Susan Eckstein has pointed out, assistance projects serve
ideological purposes by transmitting revolutionary political
values.[47] Foreign aid programs are either military or socio-
economic. Cuba first sent military advisers abroad in 1961 when
Ghana became a recipient of Cuban military assistance.
Military aid can take many forms: arms shipment; technical and
logistical support and training (in communications and training
pilots, for example); establishment of popular militias, civil
defense, and or internal security apparatus; political education
for the armed forces; and, Cuban troops. Socio-economic aid also
affects many areas: health, construction, agriculture, education,
and natural disaster relief. Aid is usually in terms of labor:
doctors, construction workers, agronomists, teachers, and other
trained personnel.

Although military internationalism remains the
centerpiece of Cuban foreign policy, developmental assistance
projects have gained importance since the mid-1970s. A Cuban
official, Carlos Martinez Salsamendi, claims that, with the
exception of Angola and Ethiopia, civilian assistance forms the
greatest part of Cuba's foreign aid to the Third World.
According to him, 14,000 Cubans have rendered civilian services
in more than 30 countries. This figure includes approximately
2,500 health professionals (1,500 of whom are doctors who,
collectively, have served in 26 countries). Salsamendi explains
that Cuban technical assistance may be either free or
compensated, depending on the country's economic situation.
Even in cases where the receiving country pays for the
technicians, such payment usually covers only living expenses
within the country; Cuba pays the regular domestic salary,
according to him. (However, there are conflicting accounts on
this point.) Bilateral or multilateral contracts for providing paid
professional personnel, Salsamendi writes, benefit the recipient
countries because Cuba places a very moderate price on the
services. For instance, a Cuban doctor with more than eight
years of experience costs about $1,100 monthly.[48]

Another dimension of Cuban aid is a scholarship program
for foreign students. As of 1984, 19,000 foreign students attended

Cuban universities, professional schools, and high schools, of whom 65% came from Africa, 22% from Latin America, 9% from the Middle East and 1% from Asia (probably from North Korea and North Vietnam).[49] Cuba also offers scholarships for short courses (basically in ideology) and for visits to the island to workers affiliated with leftist and Marxist labor unions throughout the world.

Cuban foreign policy is not above using unconventional means to achieve its ends. The most controversial of these is the backing of insurgent groups in Latin America and Africa. Since 1959, the export of revolution has meant support for guerrillas throughout Central and South America. For example, David Nolan has recently documented a connection between Havana and the Sandinistas in Nicaragua prior to 1979.[50] According to a former El Salvadoran rebel leader, Napoleon Romero, Cuban influence has permeated the movement since 1980. Montenegro claims that, through guerrillas trained in Cuba, Castro controls the insurgency in El Salvador.[51]

The use of the Fuerzas Armadas Revolucionarias outside Cuban shores in the mid-1970s was the culmination of the consolidation of the Cuban revolution and Castroite foreign relations. The development of the FAR as a domestic and external political actor parallels the historical stages of the Revolution. As a means of foreign policy, its military strength accords Cuba a privileged place in the Third World with great powers as well. For the Soviet Union, Cuba is an asset in this sphere; for the U.S., an irritant.

Cuban troop deployment has been restricted mainly to Africa, although there have been reports, some unconfirmed, of deployment elsewhere (i.e., Syria and Libya). Due to the complexity of, and the high stakes associated with, the Middle Eastern conflicts, the prospects for Cuba's military internationalism in the region should be studied.

CONCLUSION

The history of Cuban foreign relations since 1959 reflects Castroism's commitment to violent change and the extension of the lider maximo's personal influence to other areas of the world. This ideology, with its anti-U.S. bent, and its reliance on the armed forces, has served as the basis for the island's international behavior. Marxism shares certain perspectives with Castroism but is basically an instrument of the latter. Marxism unites Cuba and the U.S.S.R. in a mutually supportive alliance.

Castro's foreign policy aspirations require the assistance of a great power, since Cuba alone cannot accomplish the projects of a great power. Consequently, the Soviet-Cuban alliance should not be viewed solely as the consequence of Cuba's dependency on the U.S.S.R., although this dimension is present. Havana does depend on Moscow for economic survival and for the material base on which it can undertake military activities abroad. However, although Cuba's actions further Soviet objectives, Castro is not the Kremlin's puppet; a convergence of interests and cooperation make Cuba's ventures profitable for both states. Furthermore, Cuba is free to act in the area she knows best, the Caribbean and Latin America. As long as these actions do not threaten vital Soviet interests, Castro can pursue his own plans. The closer the targetted area is to the Soviet Union, the greater the restraint on Cuba's activities. This is the case with the Middle East as a whole, though one should analyze the situation country-by-country. Even when following a Soviet line in the region which is consonant with Castroism *per se*, Cuba seeks national gains at considerable costs and risks.

With the 1980s, Cuba's foreign policy entered a new stage. The reasons behind this shift are many, of which the more important have been the advent of a new administration in Washington and the increased domestic cost of foreign initiatives. However, Castro's international ambitions are still alive despite the setbacks. New strategies for foregn policy have been introduced.

NOTES

1. John McShane, "Cuban Foreign Policy: Global Orientations," *Latinamericanist* (May 31, 1979):1-4.

2. Robert K. Furtak in "Cuba: un cuarto de siglo de politica exterior revolucionaria," *Foro Internacional* (Abril-Junio 1985):343-361, uses a similar rubric to describe this period. He calls it "Moderacion y actitud expectativa."

3. McShane, p. 1.

4. See Justo Carrillo, "Vision and Revision: U.S.-Cuban Relations," in *Cuba: Continuity and Change,* Jaime Suchlicki, Antonio Jorge, and Damian J. Fernandez, eds., (Miami: University of Miami, 1985), pp. 165-176.

5. Robert K. Furtak, "Cuba: analisis" in *Teoria y practica de la politica exterior latinoamericana,* Gerhard Drekonja K. and Juan G. Tokatlian, eds., (Bogota: Universidad de los Andes, 1983), p. 472.

6. Cole Blasier, "The Cuban-U.S.-Soviet Triangle, Changing Angles," *Estudios Cubanos-Cuban Studies* (January 1978):2.

7. For a general account of this period see Jorge I. Dominguez *Cuba: Order and Revolution*, (Cambridge: Harvard University Press, 1975).

8. Jorge I. Dominguez, *The Success of Cuban Foreign Policy*, Center for Latin American and Caribbean Studies Occasional Papers, No. 27 (New York: New York University, 1980), p. 1.

9. William J. Durch, "The Cuban Military in Africa and the Middle East: From Algeria to Angola," *Studies in Comparative Communism* XI (Spring-Summer 1978):34-74.

10. Jorge Dominguez holds this view.

11. McShane, p. 3.

12. For an overall assessment see Carmelo Mesa-Lago and June S. Belkin, eds., *Cuba in Africa*, Latin American Monograph and Document Series, No. 3 (Pittsburgh: University of Pittsburgh, 1982).

13. For more information see Durch, and Mesa-Lago and Belkin.

14. H. Michael Erisman, *Cuba's International Relations: The Anatomy of a Nationalistic Foreign Policy*, (Boulder: Westview Press, 1985), p. 71.

15. Jorge I. Dominguez, "Cuban Foreign Policy," *Foreign Affairs* (Fall 1978):97.

16. Edward Gonzalez, "Complexities of Cuban Foreign Policy," *Problems of Communism* (November-December 1977):12.

17. Ibid., pp. 6-10. See also Jaime Suchlicki, "Is Castro Ready to Accommodate?," *Strategic Review* (Spring 1984):22-29

18. Also a rubric coined by Furtak in "Cuba: Analisis," p. 465.

19. Denial of asylum rights to Cubans who sought, in the late 1970s and early 1980s, entrance to the embassies of Costa Rica, Peru, and Venezuela damaged, at least temporarily, the relations of these countries with Havana.

20. This position is changing due to Cuba's increased military assistance to Nicaragua.

21. *Latin American Weekly Report*, 29 June 1984, p. 6.

22. See Suchlicki.

23. Andres Suarez, "Cuba: Ideology and Pragmatism," in *Cuba: Continuity and Change*, pp. 131-148.

24. For different versions of the thesis, see Nelson P. Valdes, "The Evolution of Cuban Foreign Policy in Africa" (Paper presented at the 1979 International Studies Association Meeting, Toronto, Canada); Erisman *op. cit.*; Daniel Tretiak, *Perspectives on Cuba's Relations with the Communist System: The Politics of a Communist Independent, 1959-1969* (Ann Arbor: Xerox University Microfilms); and William M. LeoGrande, "Cuban Policy in Africa," in Mesa-Lago and Belkin, eds., *op. cit.*

25. For a critique of the surrogate thesis see Falk; Erisman; and Gonzalez.

26. This discussion is based on Carmelo Mesa-Lago, "Cuban Foreign Policy in Africa: A General Framework," in *Cuba in Africa*, pp. 5-6.

27. Georges A. Fauriol, *Foreign Policy Behavior of Caribbean States: Guyana, Haiti, and Jamaica* (Lanham: United Press of America, 1984) Chapter II, pp. 11-27.

28. *Programmatic Platform*, First Congress of the Communist Party of Cuba, December, 1975. Quoted in Carlos Martinez Salsamendi, "Cuba en America Central, el Caribe y Africa," in *Cuba-Estados Unidos: dos enfoques*, Juan G. Tokatlian, ed., (Bogota: CEREC, 1984), p. 137.

29. Ibid.

30. Ibid.

31. Enrique Baloyra Herp, "Internationalism and the Limits of Autonomy: Cuba's Foreign Relations," in *Latin American Nations in World Politics*, Heraldo Munoz and Joseph S. Tulchin, eds. (Boulder: Westview Press), p. 171.

32. Ibid., p. 172.

33. Ibid.

34. Salsamendi, p. 140.

35. Ibid., p. 141.

36. Erisman, p. 8.

37. For official Cuban accounts see, for example, Ricardo Alarcon, "Relaciones entre Cuba y los Estados Unidos: pautas de conducta y opciones" in *Cuba-Estados Unidos: dos enfoques*, pp. 23-30; or Fidel Castro's speeches in *Granma*.

38. Baloyra, p. 173.

39. See Antonio Jorge, "The Transferability of Cuba's Economic Model" in *The New Cuban Presence in the Caribbean*, Barry Levine, ed., (Boulder: Westview Press, 1983)

40. Gerald J. Bender, "Angola, the Cubans, and American Anxieties," *Foreign Policy*, 31, (Spring 1978):10-11.

41. See Juan Benemelis, "Cuban Leaders and the Soviet Union," paper presented at the Seminar on Cuban-Soviet Relations, University of Miami, November 8, 1985.

42. Ibid.

43. See Dominguez *op. cit.*; LeoGrande *op. cit.*; and W. Raymond Duncan, "Funciones de Cuba en el ambito de la comunidad socialista: a la vanguardia de los intereses del Tercer Mundo?," in Tokatlian, ed., pp. 98-104.

44. Dominguez, p. 86.

45. Ibid., p. 102.

46. See W. Raymond Duncan, "Funciones de Cuba en el ambito de la comunidad socialista a la vanguardia de los intereses del Tercer Mundo," in *Cuba-Estados Unidos: dos enfoques*, Juan G. Tokatlian, ed., pp. 75-109.

47. Susan Eckstein, "Structural and Ideological Bases of Cuba's Overseas Programs," *Politics and Society* XXI, No. 1 (1982):95-121.

48. Salsamendi, p. 145.

49. Ibid.

50. David Nolan, *The FSLN: The Ideology of the Sandinistas* (Miami: University of Miami, 1984).

51. See Napoleon Romero, "Declaracion de Napoleon Romero," Club Nacional de Prensa, Washington, D.C., 11 March 1986 (mimeo).

2

Cuban Foreign Policy
in the Middle East: 1959–1987

INTRODUCTION

Cuba's policy in the Middle East is different from the island's foreign policy elsewhere in the world. Although Havana's dealings with the Arab countries share many of the trademarks of revolutionary internationalism, in the Middle East Cuba has adopted a foreign policy style uncharacteristic of traditional Cuban international relations since 1959. The new, or unprecedented, aspects of Cuba's behavior are several. First, Havana has been willing to adopt flexible positions of support to both sides of a dispute, (specifically, inter-arab conflicts); a strategy that can be called straddling the fence, or as the Cubans call it, neutrality. Second, and stemming from the first, Cuba has sought the role of mediator in the region. In the past, Havana has mediated successfully in the case of the FSLN and, not so successfully, in the case of the El Salvadoran guerrillas. These efforts have paid off in terms of greater Cuban influence over these groups. Cuba seeks to play this role whenever possible in the Middle East.

Cuba's strategy in the Middle East is a logical one for it attempts to maximize benefits and limit costs. Cuba has adapted its foreign policy in the region to the nature of Middle Eastern politics (intra-Arab factionalism and ideological diversity within the "progressive" states and groups); the Soviet regional agenda; and Cuban capability to influence events. Nevertheless, the island's involvements may result in unexpected consequences and high risks. In spite of ideological and practical flexibility, Cuba's relations with the Arab countries have revolved around several fixed concerns, many of which are consistent with larger Cuban foreign policy means and ends. Other concerns have been area specific. Among the recurrent themes of Cuba's

35

diplomacy in the area is the need for unity within Arab groups. Cuba's attempt to forge a united Arab front and end internal divisions is parallel to Castro's effort on behalf of the FSLN and on behalf of Third World brotherhood. This attempt correlates with the Cuban leadership's interest in avoiding domestic factionalism, especially after the downfall of the Maurice Bishop regime in Grenada (1983).

Cuba's initiatives in the Middle East since the 1960s, but increasingly in the 1970s and 1980s, have been devoted to bringing about Arab and Palestinian unity. In these efforts Cuba has had to walk cautiously to keep a delicate balance between opposing sides. It is in the role of mediator, negotiator, and power broker that Cuba sees herself in. The island stands to gain from this posture, while pursuing Soviet interests. Therefore, Cuba has opted for a possibly fruitful course that is also potentially dangerous and always close to failure, for neutrality is elusive in the Middle East. Cuba's record has been mixed. Yet, the island has opened doors to an expanded role in an explosive region of the world.

CUBA IN THE MIDDLE EAST: HISTORICAL BACKGROUND

The Middle East has not been a high priority item on the Cuban foreign policy agenda. Other areas, geographically, culturally, and ethnically closer to the island, have attracted most of the regime's attention. Nevertheless, various factors have combined to propel the Cuban regime into taking a more active stance in the region, not least of which is the importance of the Middle East to the Soviet Union. Some of these factors have been ideological, such as the nature of Castroism itself, an international platform which stresses Cuban solidarity with proletarian movements, as well as a self-proclaimed support for radical "anti-imperialist" forces wherever they may be found in the world. Other factors have been more pragmatic: the will to increase its leverage with the Soviet Union; the desire to establish spheres of interest of its own in the Third World, especially with oil-exporting countries that could replace the Soviets as suppliers of oil in case of a Havana-Moscow fallout; and the attempt to maximize the prestige of the Cuban Revolution and, by extension, that of its lider maximo, Fidel Castro, in other parts of the world.

From Cuba's perspective, the Middle East and Africa are one region. This connection is manifested in the Ministry of Foreign Relations, where one department is in charge of both regions. The link is the result of Cuba's experience. Algeria, an Arab-African country, was one of the first places to which revolutionary Cuba sent military and technical aid. The Arab dimension served as a unifying element between North Africa and the Middle East.

Ethnicity, however, is not the principal bond which unites Africa and the Middle East. Cuba befriends countries and groups based, not necessarily on geographical proximity or ethnic background, but on the political orientation of the regimes in power or on the potential benefits for Cuba. Havana's foreign policy claims solidarity with the Third World. Castroism calls for change and anti-Americanism. These are the driving forces of the island's international relations. Therefore, ideological affinity and pragmatic opportunism attracts the Cubans more so than regional continuity and ethnicity.

The Cubans make a distinction between black Africa and Arab Africa (and by extension the Arab-Middle East), at least in terms of race. Havana explains support for black Africa as a matter of blood unity given the black extraction of many Cubans. This claim cannot be made in reference to the Arabs. Consequently, Cuba employs the rationale of proletarian internationalism to explain its involvement in the region.

Cuban policy in the Middle East centers on the following concerns: (1) the Arab-Israeli conflict; (2) Palestinian rights and desire for a homeland; (3) the Iran-Iraq war; (4) the crisis and war in Lebanon; (5) the Organization of Petroleum Exporting Countries (OPEC) and oil; (6) support for groups-forces espousing "anti-imperialism," whether they be governments, guerrillas, terrorists, or communist parties; and, (7) pursuit and maintenance of diplomatic relations with both conservative and radical states in the region.

The countries and groups that have received the bulk of Cuban support, in both moral and material terms, are in order of priority: (1) the People's Democratic Republic of Yemen (PDRY) or South Yemen; (2) the Palestinian Liberation Organization (PLO); (3) Syria; (4) Libya; and, (5) Iraq and other minor groups such as the Lebanese Communist Party (LCP) and the Popular Liberation Front of Oman (PFLO). In the 1970s and the 1980s, Havana, in an attempt to expand its influence in the region, extended its friendship to other Middle Eastern countries and groups as well: to (1) Iran; (2) Kuwait; (3) Jordan and to (4) North Yemen. Cuba even achieved a mild rapprochement with post-Sadat Egypt.

AN OVERVIEW OF THE DEVELOPMENT
OF CUBA'S FOREIGN POLICY
IN THE MIDDLE EAST

Cuba's interest and involvement in the Middle East has grown continuously since 1959. Although Havana became involved in the region in the early 1960s, the revolutionary regime did not take a coherent position on the Arab-Israeli conflict until 1967. The island's policy was far from finalized, however, and underwent changes which signalled a willingness to follow the Soviet lead in the area and to become actively involved in Arab countries. From an initial position of ambivalence toward Isreal, the revolution became even more critical of and antagonistic to the Jewish state.

Cuba's policy vis-a-vis the Arab-Israel conflict reflects the larger trends of Cuba's conduct of international relations. Specifically, in the Middle East one can trace the development of Havana's alliance with Moscow, and also the shift from low diplomacy (that is, rhetorical rather than actual) to high diplomacy (that is, state to state relations, power politics, and mediation). The change has been a matter of emphasis rather than a complete policy reversal. In the 1960s, Cuba's efforts were concentrated on helping national liberation movements. In the 1980s, Cuba, while continuing to defend such groups, has increasingly adopted traditional forms of diplomacy to exert influence.

Revolutionary Cuba has always been concerned over the situation in the Middle East. This concern is an outgrowth of the island's big power ambitions and the active foreign policy tradition the revolution initiated. The first major policy statement on the region appeared in 1967, after the Arab-Israeli War. Up to then, and even after 1967, there was no such thing as a Cuban Middle East policy. Rather, Cuba expressed support for independence groups (i.e., in Algeria), for Israel's right to exist, and for Palestinian rights. Although a sensible posture, it put Cuba in an uncomfortable position of not pleasing either the Israeli or the Arab side. But given the low priority of the region up to 1973, this ambivalent approach was tenable.

The lack of a unified policy can be explained by several factors. First, during the initial years of the revolution, Cuba faced serious security threats which required a concentration of energy on the survival of the regime. Second, other areas closer to Cuba (namely Latin America) were of greater importance to the revolutionary leadership. And, third, the Middle East, after all, is far away from the Caribbean; is a very complex region; had little to offer Cuba then; and, did not share any major ethnic or cultural bond with the island. Moreover, there was no tradition of close relations between Cuba and the countries of the region, with the possible exception of Israel. Once the Castro regime was firmly in power and Cuba became increasingly active in international circles, Havana became more and more attracted to the Middle East.

In 1966, the Tricontinental Conference in Havana brought home the importance of the region and of the Arab world. A year later, the Cuban government took a stand on the 1967 Arab-Israeli War, calling for the withdrawl of the Israeli Armed forces from occuppied Arab territories and the guarantee of the national rights of the Palestinian people.[1]

As the Cuban-Soviet connection was formalized, the island assumed a bigger role in the Middle East. Cuba shed its policy of support of Israel for that of the Arab countries, and coordinated its activities and its policy with that of the U.S.S.R. Throughout the late 1960s and early 1970s, Cuba became ever more critical of Israeli actions and more sympathetic to the Palestinians and the Arabs. This trend culminated in 1973 when Castro announced that Cuba would break relations with Israel. Up to then, Cuba defended the Jewish homeland and compared the plight of the Jews with that of the Palestinians. According to Ricardo Alarcon, the Cuban ambassador to the UN, Cuba's opposition to prejudice "applied equally to the Palestinian people, who have been unjustly, and brutally, dispossessed of their land and to the Jewish people, who have suffered persecution for two thousand years."[2]

On several occasions, Cuba had to defend its diplomatic relations with Israel from attacks by members of the Non-Aligned Movement. In 1966, the participants of the Tricontinental Conference called for a break of relations with Israel and demanded a political, cultural, and economic boycott against it. In 1967 Fidel defended the island's refusal to adopt the Tricontinental resolution by stating that,

> Cuba's position in this painful problem is a position of principle, an intransigent position, a firm position. *Except that we do not like fig leaves.* What is Israel? An instrument of yankee imperialism, the instigator, the protector of that state. And that is why I ask those of you of the "mafia" who try to libel Cuba with such arguments: why don't you break relations with the government of the United States of America?[3]

According to official Cuban documents, Cuba's policy in the Middle East was guided by two main principles: (1) anti-imperialism and (2) anti-aggression.[4] These two tenets, allowed Cuba to justify relations with Israel (because the island viewed the U.S. as the culprit of Israeli violence against the Arabs). This posture, at the same time, allowed for criticism against the Israeli government and support for the Arab countries. Although the revolutionary government was initially sympathetic to Israel, this policy would be discarded for it stood in the way of Castro's Third World leadership aspirations. Cuba's desire to court the friendship of the powerful OPEC and Arab forces and to tow the Soviet line in the region also acted as inducements to break with Israel. In 1973, after the Yom Kippur War, Cuba, for the first time, makes Israel responsible for its own actions and equates Zionism with imperialism. Until then, Israel was but a puppet of the U.S. (Israel's policy in the Middle East had served as an additional motive to denounce U.S. imperialism.)

The end of relations with Israel in 1973 signalled the beginning of the expansion of Cuba's activities in the Middle East. Increased involvement, however, did not alter fundamentally Havana's policy toward the Arab-Israeli conflict. After the October 1973 War, Cuba continued to call for Israeli withdrawl from occupied Arab territories and for the establishment of a Palestinian homeland. What changed after 1973 was Cuba's willingness to serve as an agent of Arab unity and a power broker between Arab groups. Cuba took up the Arab cause as its own and assumed a pro-Arab leadership role in international organizations. In a 1975 Non-Aligned Movement meeting, Raul Roa, Minister of Foreign Relations, asked the members of the movement "to set, before it is too late, a clear and firm position in face of the dangerous events that are taking place in the Middle East."[5] He called on the Non-Aligned Movement to support the unconditional Israeli evacuation of the Arab lands occupied in 1967 and the guarantee of Palestinian rights. In his speech, Roa criticized the U.S.'s step by step approach to resolve the crisis. According to him, the approach only benefited the multinational oil corporations and Israel. Finally, Roa praised the "transcendental victory of OPEC in using the power of the natural resources of underdeveloped countries against the capitalist nations.[6]

Cuba's view of OPEC has been two sided. On the positive side, Cuba regarded OPEC as a victory for the Third World in its battle against the rich countries of the world and as a source of inspiration for the underdeveloped countries. Initially, Cuba hoped that OPEC would serve as a model for the producers of agricultural goods and other raw materials. Cuba also expected OPEC to offer generous aid to non-oil producing Third World states. On the negative side, Cuba has blamed OPEC for the heavy burden that the increase in oil prices have placed on poor countries. Fidel has stated that the oil price hike affected the Third World much more than it did the industrialized nations.[7] To make matters worse, OPEC did not establish a comprehensive aid package for the Third World, nor was the oil cartel a practical model for producers of other commodities to follow.

Oil is pivotal to Cuba's Middle East policy, not only because of the commodity per se, but primarily due to the link between oil and U.S. strategy in the Persian Gulf. Cuba sees the need for oil as one of the determinant factors of U.S. military presence in the Gulf, a presence which could lead to nuclear war, according to the Cubans. That was the official reason why Havana objected to the Carter Doctrine. The underlying preoccupation, however, has been the loss of Soviet influence in the area.

Cuba has acted as the defender of the Soviet Union in the Arab world. To placate the fears of many Arab countries, Havana has proclaimed that Moscow is not a threat to the Arab world. The real enemy, according to Cuba, lurks in U.S. imperialism and Zionism. Castro's policy in the region has been construed in opposition to U.S. policy. Cuba is against U.S. presence in the Middle East (especially, U.S. military bases); opposes U.S.-inspired peace negotiations; and, supports the Arabs against the Israelis. The Cubans see themselves, and the Soviets, as the natural allies of the Arab peoples and point to the anti-Americanism of Arab masses. Furthermore, according to Cuba, while no Arab country can define its foreign policy without taking into consideration the Palestinian problem, the U.S. sees the Palestinian issue as marginal. Cuba and the Soviet Union, on the contrary, have made the creation of a Palestinian state an integral part of their proposals for the resolution of the Arab-Israeli crisis.

The convergence of interests between the Soviet-Cuban and the Arab position is clear. For instance, Cuba joined the Soviet Union and most Arab countries in condemning the Camp David Accords (1978), the U.S. negotiated peace treaty between Israel and Egypt. Cuban opposition to the Accords stemmed from what Cuba saw as the U.S. effort to divide the Arab countries by way of a separate settlement between Israel and Egypt. The Camp David accords left out two of the island's main concerns in the Middle East: Palestinian and Soviet interests. Cuba adopted the Arab position that Egypt was the traitor of Arab unity. (From then on Cuba added the concept of reactionary Arab state to its list of enemies of the Arab cause. In the late 1970s and in the 1980s, Cuba applied the label of reactionary Arab state with increasing frequency to countries other than Egypt, especially Saudi Arabia).

In spite of ideological rigidity at home and the partnership with Moscow, Havana's policy in the Middle East has shown flexibility and pragmatism. Cuba has been willing to embrace movements, groups, and countries which do not espouse Marxism-Leninism. The only common bond between these various groups and Marxism-Leninism is an anti-status quo posture, and, in most cases, strident anti-Americanism. The most interesting example of this is Castro's perception of and support for the Islamic revolution in Iran (See section on Iran). What at first appears as flexibility and pragmatism on Cuba's part (i.e., acceptance of a revolution which in more ways than one has been reactionary and anti-Soviet) may reveal the ideological underpinnings of Castro's foreign policy, anti-Americanism and social change through violent revolution.

In the 1980s, Cuba's policy in the Middle East has kept its basic features unchanged. What has changed is the emphasis Castro has given the region in the mid-1980s, after a lull in the early 1980s. The new emphasis on the Arab countries can be seen in the reorganization of the North Africa and Middle East Section of Cuba's Ministry of Foreign Relations and in the wave of activities with, and attention to, Arab groups and countries. The growing importance of the Middle East on the Cuban foreign policy agenda was evident in Castro's speech in the 1983 Non-Aligned Summit Meeting in which Middle Eastern issues (the massacres in Lebanon, the Palestinian problem, and the danger of war in the region) were the first to be discussed.[8] During 1985 and 1986, all the major Arab countries visited Cuba and-or signed cooperation agreements with the island.

In 1986-1987, Cuba actively sought Palestinian and Arab unity by acting as a power broker between different factions. The purpose of this new diplomatic offensive was very specific, to lay down the pre-requisites for an international peace conference in which all the interested parties in the Arab-Israeli conflict would come together. The idea of a peace conference in which the Soviet Union would participate has been at the top of the Soviet Middle East agenda. Cuba has attempted mediation to help the plans materialize. Havana's policy of mediation and neutrality puts the island in an enviable position to exert its influence and expand its role in regional politics.

STAGES OF CUBA'S POLICY IN THE REGION

Cuba's relations with countries of the Middle East fall roughly into five periods: (1) 1959-1973 - Autonomous foreign policy, marked by a dual relationship with both Israel and the Arab states; (2) 1973-1977 - Accommodation to the Soviet line; anti-Israeli policy combined with relations with "progressive states;" (3) 1977-1980 - Activist policy in the region, expanded role and diplomatic relationships; (4) 1981-1985 - Cautious involvement, restrained activism, emphasis on socio-economic cooperation; and, (5) 1986 to present (1987) - New diplomatic offensive with emphasis on mediation.

Autonomy-Dual Policy: 1959-1973

During the first year following the success of the Cuban revolution, Cuba continued Batista's policy of friendly relations

with the Israeli government.[9] The Cuban press gave
sympathetic coverage to most events in Israel; an Israeli charge
d' affaires was stationed in Havana (February 1960), and, in
return, the new revolutionary government sent Ricardo
Subirana y Lobo to serve as consul. Several technical
cooperation projects were initiated, although trade between both
countries remained small. After 1960, cordial relations with
Israel deteriorated into diplomatic ambivalence: anti-Israeli
rhetoric began to be heard at the same time that the Cuban
government gave verbal support to Arab causes in international
pronouncements.

The shift can be explained by several factors: the
rapprochement which took place between Havana and Moscow
after 1968; the ascension to positions of power by members of the
Partido Socialista Popular (PSP), the old Cuban Communist Party,
a group which was not as pro-Israel as the members of the July
26 Movement or the *Directorio Estudiantil* had been; and, Castro's
ideological penchant for favoring revolutionary causes. Years
later, Cuba's attempt to become a leader in the Non-Aligned
Movement and a standard-bearer for the Third World, required
it to alter its relations with Israel. Up until 1973, Havana's
policy toward the Middle East differed from that of Moscow,
demonstrating a degree of independence in world affairs that
would be reduced thereafter.

From 1959 to 1973, contacts with countries and groups in
the Middle East were few. Except for Algeria, Havana did not
make extensive commitments to Arab nations or groups prior to
the early 1970s. Algeria was a special case, as Cuba had provided
guerrilla training and health services for the Algerian National
Liberation Front during its war for independence as early as
1960. Later, in 1963, Cuba sent two shipments of arms to the
Algerians during their border war with Morocco. Although the
evidence is not clear, some sources claim that Cuban troops even
fought against the Moroccans. Allegedly this provoked Morocco
into breaking relations with Havana.[10]

By the mid-1960s, Cuba's drift toward active support for
radical Arab causes had become increasingly apparent. Arab
delegations visited the island and received warm welcomes.
Joint Cuban-Arab declarations called for establishment of a
Palestinian homeland; editorials in the official press sided with
the Palestinians and against Israel; Cuba lobbied in the U.N. for
Arab regimes; and the PLO was granted revolutionary
legitimacy. Castro viewed the PLO as a progressive Arab force,
opposing reactionary forces. This support, however, was verbal
rather than substantive. Yoram Shapira concluded that Cuban
support for the Palestinians was meager during the 1960s,
although it increased thereafter. Shapira indicated that Cubans

trained Palestinian guerrillas and were involved in combat operations in the area.[11]

K.S. Karol reports, based on interviews with Castro, that the Cuban leader opposed Israeli policies of aggression but was also critical of the PLO for pledging to annihilate an entire people. According to Karol, Castro blamed the U.S. for the conflict in the Middle East.[12] Castro's statements typified the conflicting dual policies of this period. Havana tried to balance relations with Israel and with Arab groups at the same time. In international conferences held on the island, the juggling act was difficult. The 1966 Tricontinental Conference of Solidarity of Peoples was characterized by Cuba's non-committal acquiescence to anti-Zionist resolutions. In the 1968 International Cultural Congress held in Havana, Cuban delegates had to mobilize other participants to remove a strongly worded anti-Israeli resolution from the agenda, which threatened to divide the conference.[13]

In the U.N., Cuba's voting pattern on Israeli issues changed perceptibly after the overthrow of Batista, who had consistently exhibited a pro-Israel stance. In the early 1960s, the regime criticized Israel but maintained cordial relations. By the 1967 War, Cuba's behavior in the U.N. had become actively anti-Israeli. It was not until after 1973, that Israel became a principal target of Cuba's anti-imperialist campaign. The delay in the Cuba's official break with Israel is in part explained by Nasser's animosity toward Castro. On the one hand, Nasser blocked the Cuban leader's entrance into the region. On the other, Castro used the Israeli card as pressure on the Arabs. He would not break with Israel until the Arab countries were ready to accept Castro in the region.[14]

*Accommodation to the
Soviet Line: 1973-1977*

Cuba's relations with the Middle East entered into a new stage after 1973. The change is signaled by Havana's decision to break diplomatic relations with Israel. The move was motivated primarily by Cuba's accommodation with the U.S.S.R. and by pressure from Arab states. The five year delay between alignment with Moscow, the break with Israel, and Cuba's active involvement in the Middle East reflected two basic phenomena. First, in 1968 the island did not have a military establishment equipped (professionally or materially) to enter into overseas activities. The required military coordination between the Soviets and the Cubans that was the prelude to military internationalism occurred after 1968, setting the stage for Cuba's entrance into the Arab countries. Second, 1973 was a year of explosive tension in the region, leading to the October War and OPEC economic warfare. The Soviets, sensing this, encouraged the Cubans to assert themselves in the region. Castro, realizing not only the importance of the area, but of the oil-exporting Arab countries as well as took the opportunity. It was a good time to do so given Cuba's failure in Latin America.

Castro announced his decision to terminate relations with Israel at the Algiers conference of the Non-Aligned Movement (1973) as a way to polish his revolutionary image. In Algiers, the Cuban leader had been under attack from Muammar Qaddafi who claimed that Cuba had no place attending the summit since, as an ally of the Soviet Union, it was not truly non-aligned. Castro refuted these charges contending that the Soviet Union was the natural ally of the Third World since she was not imperialist or capitalist. In return for rapprochement with the Arab world and wider acceptance in the Non-Aligned Movement, Castro broke relations with Israel.

In the Middle East, Castro's policy combined pragmatism with ideology. It was pragmatic to become useful to the Soviets. It was also pragmatic to cultivate the friendship of oil-producing, capital-exporting countries. Cuba, heavily dependent on Soviet oil and finance, might need her Arab friends in the future. Ideologically, OPEC fit nicely with Fidel's own agenda of confrontation against the capitalist world.

After changes in the FAR that made possible international military missions, Havana put into practice its new interest. Cuba established military programs in South Yemen (1973) and Syria (1973-4). Havana opened an embassy in Kuwait in 1973 and sent a military mission to Iraq in 1976. Cuban troops were reported in Syria during the October 1973 Yom Kippur War.[15] Additionally, Cuba sponsored socio-economic projects in these countries.

Activism and Role Expansion: 1977-1980

The third stage in the development of Cuba's Middle Eastern policy starts in March 1977 when Castro toured Africa and attempted to mediate the Ethiopian-Somalian imbroglio. Castro's proposal was based on the formation of an anti-imperialist federation composed of Ethiopia, Somalia, South Yemen, and autonomous Ogaden and Eritrea. Although the effort failed, Castro's mediation underscored Cuba's diplomatic commitment to the region. Intermediation reflected a new foreign policy style, one which assumed a great power stance, both by deploying troops and by initiating a diplomatic offensive.

At the invitation of Qaddafi, Fidel spent 10 days in Libya during his African tour. The reason for Qaddafi's overture was that Qaddafi's isolation in the Arab world and his need to revamp his revolutionary plans. It was the first time the Cuban leader visited Libya, marking a reconciliation between Qaddafi and Castro after years of friction within the Non-Aligned Movement. The Libyan rapprochement reinforced Castro's legitimacy within the Arab world and opened the door for further initiatives in the Middle East. Since 1977, Libya has been one of Havana's faithful allies. Bilateral relations proliferated in the form of various cooperative ventures in the Middle East, in Central America, and in the Caribbean. (Chapter 4 studies Cuban-Libyan ties in detail).

Cuba's activities in Angola and Ethiopia produced sufficient prestige to encourage the island to expand its foreign policy on a broader scale. Not only had the regime proved itself capable of standing by its friends militarily, but also proved that it could be a source of developmental aid for other Third World countries. With these credentials and important allies in the Middle East, Cuba was ready to develop its contacts. In turn, the Arab countries were ready to respond to Cuba's overtures.

Moderate Activism:
1981-1985

Role expansion and activism in the region suffered a temporary setback in 1980 by four events: (1) Castro's endorsement of the Soviet invasion of Afghanistan; (2) Cuba's loss of the Non-Aligned chairmanship; (3) Havana's failure to mediate the Iran-Iraq conflict; and (4) the election of Ronald Reagan as president of the United States. Domestic problems in the island and in the Soviet Union also worked against deepening commitment in the area. Nevertheless, the early 1980s saw a moderate expansion of Cuban relations with Middle Eastern actors. While the military component has remained relatively stable since the 1970s, Cuban socio-economic assistance and bilateral and multilateral diplomatic cooperation increased in the early 1980's. (See Table 1) Trade has not been an important dimension in Cuban-Middle Eastern ties, as of yet, although an undetermined amount of Arab oil is said to reach Cuba.[16]

The New Internationalism:
1985 to the Present (1987)

The mid and late 1980s have seen a resurgence of Cuban diplomacy in the Middle East. The island's increasing concern for the region followed a series of unhappy circumstances for Cuba. The new offensive has been evidenced by several developments and is guided by Cuba's interest in mediating Arab unity and laying the ground work for Soviet interests.

The island's inability to forge unity among Arab factions was not only a source of frustration, but a major concern for Havanas' policy in the area. The fear of fraticidal battles materialized once again in the January 1986 civil war in South Yemen. Both Cuba and the Soviet Union were caught by surprise when personal rivalries within the leaders of the PDRY government erupted into full fledged violence. During the confrontation, *Granma* called for an end to the struggle, claiming that fraticidal violence only furthered the aim of Israel, the U.S., and the reactionary Arab states. Although there is no hard evidence, one can speculate that it is not unlikely that Cuba tried to mediate between the warring sides in Aden. This would fall in line with previous Cuban behavior in that country. Factionalism in the PDRY threatened the island directly, for throughout the 1970s the Cuban military mission and the Cuban embassy (headed by separate entitites in the Cuban foreign policy establishment--one military, the other civilian) sided with different contenders in the struggle for power (See Section on the PDRY).

The events in South Yemen alerted the Cubans to the risks associated with involvement in the Middle East. After the South Yemen civil war, the Cuban leadership reorganized the North Africa and Middle East Section of the Ministry of Foreign Relations; named a new section chief (Ulises Estrada, former ambassador to the PDRY); reformulated its priorities in the area; and commited itself to a new diplomatic offensive. The strategy adopted after 1985 combined old elements of Cuba's policy with new ones. Support for Arab unity; neutrality in inter-Arab conflicts; and, opposition of Israel were reemphasized. In 1986 and 1987 Cuba's actions reflected a strong commitment to those principles. Unity among Arabs and the end of factionalism became the banner of Cuba's initiatives in the area.

After the Yemen debacle in January 1986, Cuba adopted a dual track policy. The first track was to bring the different factions of the PLO together, specifically by mediating the conflict between George Habash of the Front for the Liberation of Palestine, a hardline group, and Yasser Arafat of the Al Fatah, the majority and more moderate faction of the PLO.

Both groups have had longstanding contacts in Havana. In the first half of 1987, at a time when the PLO was attempting to cement a common position that would enable them to participate in an international Middle East peace conference, Habash and Arafat sent representatives to meet with Castro. The second track of Cuba's policy was to maintain an equidistant position in Arab conflicts, namely the Iran-Iraq War and inter-state and inter-group conflicts.

By fostering unity among groups and, at the same time, sustaining neutrality, Cuba enhanced its position as a potential mediator of inter-Arab disputes. This is the best policy option for it reduces the risks of losing influence among the Arab states while increasing potential influence in the region. This course of action carries benefits for the Soviets as well. In 1986 and 1987, Cuba's policy in the Middle East has been closely orchestrated with Soviet policy. The synchronization of Cuban-Soviet policy is seen in both countries' call for an international peace conference in which, among others, the PLO and the Soviet Union would participate. In short, Cuba has expanding its diplomatic involvement in the region as well as attempting to strengthen trade and commercial ties with the Arab world.

CUBAN-SOVIET OBJECTIVES
AND POLICY TENETS
IN THE MIDDLE EAST

Cuba is both an independent and a dependent actor in the Middle East. While the relative power vacuum in Africa granted Cuba room to act and react, in the Arab countries greater constraints are present due to the involvement of the two superpowers. Whereas African states had witnessed the arrival of Cuban troops and personnel since the early 1960s, it was not until a decade later that Cubans reached the Middle East. Timing is quite revealing for two reasons: first, since the initial years of Castro's rise to power, the Cuban leaders expounded historical, cultural, and ethnic affinities between the island and Africa. On the other hand, ties with the Middle East, if at all present, were weak. (It is important to remember that during this period Cuba supported Israel). Second, the quality of Cuban-Soviet relations was strikingly different in the 1960s than in the 1970s. The partnership with the U.S.S.R. influenced Cuban activities abroad, especially in the Middle East where Soviet stakes are high.

In the opening speech to the First Congress of the PCC in 1975, Castro expressed his interest in "that decisive part of the world" where the actions of "the United States, through the Zionist State of Israel ... threaten the southern flank of the

Soviet Union."[17] In practice, since 1973, the tenets of Cuban policy in the region parallel those of Soviet policy:[18] (1) support for Arab states in their efforts against Israel; (2) support for the PLO and a Palestinian homeland; (3) creation of a regional front against the United States, capitalism, and imperialism; (4) establishment of diplomatic relations with Arab states, both radical and conservative; (5) contact with and support to local Communist parties and organizations; (6) foster the spread of socialist ideology; and, (7) support for terrorist groups.

Rubinstein has summarized the general characteristics of Soviet policy in the Arab world. Not surprisingly, they apply to Cuba's behavior in the region.

> First, the Soviet Union pursues a differentiated policy that is sensitive to constraints and opportunities ... [to] maintain good relations with both sides in the quagmire of Arab politics.
> Second, strategic considerations and not ideological preferences have shaped Soviet diplomacy.
> Third, the Soviet Union has been a reliable patron-protector.
> Fourth, Moscow has not been adverse to intensifying local arms race. It knows that arms are its principal attraction for anti-Western Arab leaders.
> Finally, running through Soviet policy and interest in the Arab East is the central aim of eroding the United States' position and influence.[19]

Rubinstein claims that the Soviet Union is becoming increasingly venturesome in the region, and has shown itself willing to use military power to exploit conflicts and secure gains. The Russians employ Cuba in this context. Like Moscow, Cuba" is playing a shrewd game of diplomatic roulette in the Arab world. Like a seasoned gambler it backs several numbers at the same time, hoping to parlay a small stake into a big payoff and prevent the United States from coming out ahead."[20]

Cuban, and Soviet, actions in the region are motivated by both defensive and offensive concerns. Although the internationalization of Middle Eastern conflicts is not necessarily a zero-sum game, any advance Havana and Moscow make by expanding and deepening influence could represent a loss for the United States.

However, it would be misleading to portray the Soviets solely as an anti-status quo power zealously attempting to upset the balance of things. On the contrary, the Soviets are prudent calculators seeking to maximize gains and limit risks. In the past years they have mananged to juggle several conflicting spheres of interests (maintaining relations with both moderate and radical states) quite successfully without jeopardizing any. With Castro's consent, Cuban forces and aid can serve as proxy for Soviet policies without the Soviets being directly involved. Cubans, therefore, can act as Soviet point men in the foreign policy field. Cuba's close relations with the most revolutionary of the regimes allows the Soviets the option of soothing the fears of the more moderate states with minimal cause for friction.

Overall, Fidel's actions work well for the Soviet side of the Middle Eastern ledger. In the event of military showdown, well-armed friends willing to fight are an asset. Cuban diplomatic mediation (as in the Iran-Iraq war) tends to work to the Soviet advantage. At the same time, an over eager Cuban initiative in the region could present the Kremlin with an unwanted or undesirable situation where difficult choices might have to be made. This has not been the case thus far.

CUBA'S ENTRANCE INTO THE MIDDLE EAST: THE REGION, SOVIET PERSPECTIVES IN 1973, AND THE ATTRACTION OF CUBAN FOREIGN POLICY

The situation in the Middle East in the early 1970's resembled the calm before the storm. First, war between Egypt and Israel had been brewing for years and was now a matter of time. Egypt's new president, Anwar Sadat, believed that only an all out confrontation would lead both sides to the negotiating table. The Arab countries, however, were divided over the appropriate timing for war against Israel. Second, the Soviets opposed Sadat's war plans as well. The Six Day War (1967) had shown Israel's superior military power. Moreover, confrontation with Israel could lead to war with the U.S. Third, the death of Nasser in 1970 put into question Egypt's closeness to the Soviet Union. A shift in Egyptian politics would have important repercussions on the whole region and on the Arab-Israeli conflict.[21]

The Soviets, faced with this panorama, tried to delay the Egyptians' decision to go to war. In so doing, the Soviets disengaged themselves from Sadat, partly voluntarily and partly by imposition. The Kremlin recognized that involvement in a regional conflict of this sort risked *detente* and the Soviet Union's standing in the Middle East.[22] Consequently, the Soviet leaders adopted a policy of "aid and support [for the Arabs] but no responsibility."[23] It is within this rationale of indirect Soviet activism that Cubans (and East Europeans) became useful to the Kremlin. Cuban military missions would improve the Arabs' ability to fight the Israelis. This would further Soviet interests without the risks involved in direct Soviet participation.

The use of Cuba in the Middle East had domestic political value for the Soviet leaders as well. Aid programs to the Third World were not popular among the party and state bureaucracy.[24] Chanelling assistance through a third party (in this case, Cuba) was an incentive for the Soviet leaders to turn to Fidel and to encourage the entrance of Cuba into the Middle East.

Cuba's involvement in the Middle East has been facilitated by three factors: the personality of Fidel Castro; the image of Cuba as a model of socio-economic and political development; and, Havana's contact with and leverage vis-a-vis the Soviet Union. The power of these factors lie in their attractiveness to the Arab world. These three factors, on occasion, however, have been liabilities rather than assets.

Fidel Castro has facilitated Cuba's policy in the Middle East in two ways: (1) by his stature as an international revolutionary; and, (2) by giving a personal touch to foreign policy in a region where personalism is a strong political force. As head of state and chief foreign policymaker, he meets with Arab delegations visiting the island. Many of these Arab leaders have paid homage to Fidel. Furthermore, Fidel's preeminent position in Cuban politics since 1959 has provided continuity in foreign policy and a central focus for foreign leaders. His power, his personality, as well as his achievements, have been powerful forces in Cuba's foreign policy.

In spite of Fidel's charisma and influence throughout the Arab world, he has encountered opposition from Arab leaders, even among some who have professed radical ideologies. Gammal Abdel Nasser of Egypt looked cautiously at Cuba and tried to block Fidel's incursion into Arab politics. Muammar Qaddafi challenged Fidel's position in the Third World movement, Cuba's involvement in other countries, and denounced the island's relations with the Soviet Union. Both Nasser and Qaddafi rivaled Fidel for power within the Non-Aligned Movement and resented his increasing interest in Arab countries. Nasser and Qaddafi are known for their pan-Arabism which theoretically, at least, leaves little room for outsiders such as Castro.

If the past is any indication, the future may present similar problems. First, the younger generation of Arab leaders may see Castro in a different light. Furthermore, who is to say that today's sympathizers will not become tomorrow's antagonists? A reevaluation of Castro's intentions in the region as well as of his ties to Moscow may undermine Cuba's standing in the region. Second, Castro's position as kingpin of Cuba's foreign policy presents another set of future problems. What will happen to Cuba's influence in the area once Castro is no longer in power? What course can the Arabs expect from Havana after succession? The uncertainty of transfer of power should worry any country who has close relations with the island.

The image of Castro as the Third World revolutionary goes hand in hand with another image, that of Cuba as a model of socio-economic and political development. Castro and the fruits of socialism are two features which have attracted attention to the island. Throughout the Third World many have looked up to Fidel for leadership and to Cuba for an alternative development strategy. The Cuban leadership has promoted the notion of Cuba as a model. The island has become a showcase of socialist development. This has gained Cuba the admiration of many groups and countries, but it has brought dilemmas as well. The island has found itself in a difficult position. The Cuban economy has failed in meeting development goals, in freeing itself from dependency on Soviet aid and, in solving the problem of inefficiency and low labor productivity.

Cuba's relationship with the Soviet Union is the third factor which has facilitated the island's involvement in the Middle East. The Soviet Union has encouraged Cuba's policy in many ways, from supporting Cuba's mediating role in the Iran-Iraq War, to supplying the military aid necessary for the establishment of Cuban military missions in the Arab countries. Some authors have pointed to the foreign policy division of labor that exists between the Soviet Union and its allies. Such tasks as the organization of neighborhood committees and training in the use of Soviet weaponry have been delegated to Cuba. In a less direct way, the Cuban-Soviet connection has increased Cuba's influence in the region. Havana's leverage vis-a-vis Moscow has put Cuba in the enviable position of acting as intermediary between the Kremlin and Arab groups. Cuba's lobby function in favor of a Middle Eastern country has been best documented in the case of the People's Democratic Republic of Yemen. Furthermore, as discussed above, there are indications that Third World leaders feel more comfortable dealing with the Cubans than dealing with the Soviets.

Although the link to the Soviet Union has produced benefits in terms of expanding Cuba's reach in the Middle East, the Soviet connection is to blame for costs as well. Arab countries (i.e., Egypt, Libya, and others) have questioned Cuba's non-alignment, claiming that the island is a Soviet puppet. Havana's closeness to Moscow makes the island's activities in the region suspicious to conservatives, moderates, radical nationalists, and Islamic fundamentalists who do not regard the U.S.S.R. favorably. As a result, Cuba's role as mediator may be at risk. The island treads a thin line between: (1) serving Soviet interests (and reaping rewards for doing so); (2) pursuing its own agenda; (3) supporting its friends; and, (4) remaining neutral in the many inter-Arab conflicts and not appearing to be the mouthpiece of Soviet interests.

THE ARAB VIEW OF CUBA

The countries with whom Cuba enjoys the closest relations are those who have maintained longstanding cordial relations with the Soviet Union. Although Arab states, including radical regimes, have been cautious in their contacts with Moscow, and generally hostile to domestic communism, they display several characteristics in common with Havana: (1) anti-Westernism, specifically anti-United States; (2) anti-Israel and anti-Zionism; (3) pro-Palestinian homeland and pro-PLO; (4) support for the cause of Non-Alignment and other Third World interests; (5) centralized authoritarian governments; and, (6) reliance on the armed forces as main pillar of power.

An example of ideological convergence was provided at the Sixth Nonaligned Summit Meeting, held in Havana in September 1979. During the meeting, Arab states first demanded the expulsion of Egypt in retaliation for its negotiation of a separate peace treaty with Israel (since the Movement had defined Zionism as a form of racism); second, declared Israel guilty of imperialism; and third, called for a need for a comprehensive peace settlement for the region. Egypt was perceived to have betrayed the Movement by signing the Camp David Accords. Moderates within the conference, led by Yugoslavia, defended Egypt's right to membership regardless of its stance vis-a-vis Israel. Writing on this subject, Erisman concluded that:

> In principle, the *Fidelistas* supported the radical Arabs because their views on defining non-alignment were practically identical. Moreover, very bad blood had characterized Cuban-Egyptian relations ever since the 1978 Belgrade meeting. But in practice Havana was more circumspect. The farthest it was willing to go was to call for censuring the Sadat regime and to promote retribution short of ouster. This moderation was rooted in pragmatism ...[25]

The Final Declaration of the Sixth NAM Summit blamed the U.S. for preventing a just and encompassing solution to the Middle East crisis (paragraph 100), and for aiding Israel's attacks on Lebanon which led to the genocide of Lebanese and Palestinians (paragraph 117).[26]

In a speech at the International Conference of Solidarity with the Struggles of the African and Arab Peoples Against Imperialism and Reaction held in Addis Ababa, 14 September 1978, Castro expressed views on the Middle East similar to those of the Final Declaration:

> The imperialists persist in supporting the Zionist reactionaries and their occupation of Arab territories, in particular, of Palestinian territories.
> The Camp David talks are a desperate attempt to maintain the diplomacy of conceding the Arab and Palestinian peoples their rights in partial installments, and to prevent the presence of the Arab countries and their allies at the Geneva negotiations.[27]

Faced with this panorama, Castro called for a unified front against the imperialists.

Castro's pro-Arabism has gained him the admiration of Arab leaders. They have endowed Castro with heroic qualities. He is portrayed as the guerrilla fighter who revolutionized Cuban society, established an egalitarian system at home, and defended Third World causes abroad despite U.S. antagonism. Admiration for Castro is apparent in official Arab pronouncements. Qaddafi, at one time Castro's enemy, lauded the Cuban leader for being a revolutionary of global stature.[28]

For Middle Eastern countries, Cuba serves more practical functions beyond the one of international lobbyist. Relations with Cuba, including military training missions and socio-economic projects, reduces the Arab countries' dependence on the Soviets. Havana can provide technicians to instruct the Arab military on the use of Soviet weaponry, assist in the creation of a security apparatus, and in the establishment of para-military forces. By doing this, the Arab states, traditionally cautious in their dealings with Moscow, reduce their fear and the risks of Soviet penetration of their societies. In the field of construction, agronomy, education, and health Cuba is a provider of services that Arab countries are seeking. Furthermore, as pointed out before, there are indications that it is easier to deal with the Cubans than with the Soviets. Of course, Cuban assistance is by no means an adequate replacement for Soviet-Arab relations. In the final analysis Cuba is a poor country, itself dependent on the U.S.S.R.

The Arab countries prominence in the international arena since 1973 has led them to pursue active foreign policies. In their attempt to develop global contacts, the rich Arab countries (such as Saudi Arabia and Kuwait) have devoted political and economic resources to Latin America.[29] In the UN, the Latin American vote is necessary to achieve a majority.

Cuba can serve as a bridge between radical groups or states and other regimes and groups. Such has been the case with the Sandinistas in Nicaragua and Arab states. Castro had had contacts with the Frente Sandinista de Liberacion Nacional (Sandinista Front for National Liberation, FSLN) since the 1960s, so he was able to serve as contact between the Sandinistas and Libya. The extent of this bridge linkage will be discussed below.

IMPLEMENTATION OF CUBAN FOREIGN POLICY IN THE MIDDLE EAST

In the Middle East, Cuba has followed traditional methods for implementing foreign policy:

(1) Commercial and financial cooperation in which skilled and semi-skilled laborers are sent abroad. Trade and loan agreements are signed. Of special importance are the health, education, agricultural, and construction sectors;

(2) Military cooperation--Cuban advisers and technicians provide training on the use of Soviet weaponry and service Soviet equipment;

(3) Political cooperation and state-building support--Cuba has helped to organize the security apparatus of some countries and to develop popular political organizations similar to those established on the island since 1959, specifically people's militias and neighborhood committees for the defense of the regime; and,

(4) Regional and international support--In international and regional forums Cuba stands beside its friends. The regime espouses tercermundismo and supports anti-Israel resolutions in the U.N. and other organizations.

Cuba entered the Middle East by sending military assistance to Algeria in the early 1960s and by establishing military missions in several countries in the early and mid-1970s (Syria, South Yemen, Ethiopia, Iraq). The Middle East and Africa are the first recipients of FAR personnel and programs. Military diplomacy ushered in an era of cooperation between Castro's regime and key Middle Eastern governments and groups. Before then, contacts were limited, and largely uninstitutionalized.

Writing on the decision to send Cuban troops to Syria in 1973, Benemelis writes:

> During the Yom Kippur War, the Soviet requested the presence of Cuban tank units. Osmani Cienfuegos takes charge of coordinating these operations in Syria. A Cuban presence remains in the Golan Heights until the beginning of 1975 . . .[30]

TABLE 2.1
An Overview of Cuba's Relations with Middle Eastern Countries and Groups (1985)

	EMBASSY (YEAR)	MILITARY MISSION	SOCIO-ECONOMIC PROJECTS	ESTIMATED NO. OF CUBAN PERSONNEL	LEVEL OF INTERACTION & CUBAN INFLUENCE	OTHER
EGYPT			HEALTH AGRICULTURE		LOW	TRADE
IRAN	X (1985)				LOW	MEDIATION IRAN-IRAQ; NON-ALIGNED AFFAIRS.
IRAQ	X	X (1976)	CONSTRUCTION HEALTH SPORTS POLICE SQUADS	2,000	MODERATE	MEDIATION IRAN-IRAQ; NON-ALIGNED AFFAIRS; TRAINING OF PLO.
LEBANON	X				LOW	LEBANESE COMMUNIST PARTY
LIBYA	X (1977)	X	CONSTRUCTION HEALTH EDUCATION MILITARY AND PARA-MILITARY INSTITUTION & TRAINING	2,000	MODERATE	JOINT SUPPORT FOR GUERRILLAS AND TERRORIST GROUPS; BRIDGE TO NICARAGUA & THE CARIBBEAN
JORDAN	NON-RESIDENT AMBASSADOR				VERY LOW OR NONE	
KUWAIT	X (1973)		COMMUNICATIONS		LOW	
OMAN						SUPPORT FOR NFLD
PLO	FULL DIPLOMATIC STATUS; EMBASSY IN HAVANA	JOINT TRAINING IN CUBA, IRAQ, LIBYA & PDRY	SCHOLARSHIPS		MODERATE-HIGH	BRIDGE TO NICARAGUA; LOBBYIST AT UN & NON-ALIGNED MOVEMENT; INTERACTION WITH SOVIET UNION; MEDIATION BETWEEN PLO FACTIONS
PDRY	X	X (1973)	CONSTRUCTION HEALTH, MEDIA CULTURE, MILITARY & PARA-MILITARY INSTITUTION & TRAINING AGRICULTURE & FISHING	700-800	HIGH	TROOPS; FAR INFLUENCE; INFLUENCE IN DOMESTIC & REGIONAL POLITICS
SYRIA	X	X (1973)	CONSTRUCTION HEALTH PARA-MILITARY	300-500	MODERATE	TROOPS DEPLOYED 1973
YEMEN ARAB REPUBLIC	AMBASSADOR WITH RESIDENCE IN KUWAIT SERVES JOINTLY				VERY LOW	

Benemelis adds that "at Soviet insistence, there is also distribution of substantial military aid to South Yemen, as well as the training of Dhofar's guerrillas in Oman, at the specific request of Iraqi and Palestinian communists."[31] The zenith of Cuba's military involvement in the region was between the mid and the late 1970s (See Table 1). As Angola and Ethiopia drained much of the island's military energy, commitment in the Middle East waned, being replaced, at least partially, by socioeconomic projects and conventional diplomacy.

Complementing the formal channels of foreign policy-making and execution (Fidel Castro; members of the ruling elite, such as Osmani Cienfuegos, Isidoro Malmierca, Carlos Rafael Rodriuez, Levi Farah, and Jesus Montane Oropesa; and the state and Party bureaucracy, i.e., the Africa and Middle East Section of the Ministry of Foreign Relations and the FAR), the Cuban government has established a series of "friendship committees" and "brigades" sponsored by the *Instituto Cubano de Amistad con los Pueblos* (Cuban Institute of Friendship with Peoples, or ICAP). ICAP's principal committee on the Middle East is the Cuban-Arab Friendship Committee. ICAP also sponsors individual country committees; for example, the Cuban-Syrian Friendship Committee. These organizations serve as hosts for Middle Eastern visitors, plan special activities (such as lectures); and, organize internationalist workers brigades in different fields (health, education, construction, and others). The brigades are established jointly with the work centers. The *brigadistas internacionales* (international brigadeers) travel to the selected country to assist in development projects.

The Friendship Committees and the international brigades fuse ideological and pragmatic objectives. Proletarian internationalism considers the worker as both agent and recipient of foreign policy actions. Popular participation at the level of hosts and *brigadistas* offer this form of participation and serves as mechanism for political *conscientizacion* (consciousness-raising) regarding the Third World and the duties of Cuban citizens. In pragmatic terms, the committees provide good international public relations, a fundamental pre-requisite for effective diplomacy.[32]

Finally, the Arab Union of Cuba serves as an information clearinghouse on the Arab world. It sponsors special activities dealing with Arab culture and politics and hosts Arab visitors to Cuba.

CUBA-MIDDLE EAST TRADE

Although Cuba is interested in increasing its volume of trade and in securing new trade partners, both to fuel economic growth and to reduce dependence on the Soviet Union, the island's foreign policy is not dictated by economic considerations. Economic objectives are, at best, of secondary importance in the island's international agenda. With the exception of Cuba's relations with the two superpowers there is no pre-determined cause and effect between quality of relations and quantity of commerce. Cuba's relations with a nation might be cool and speckeled with conflict, yet a healthy trade relationship may exist (as is the case of Cuba and China). On the contrary, Havana may enjoy warm relations with another country, including vast influence on the regime in power, but trade between the two might be minimal due to structural economic conditions (as is the case of Cuba and the PDRY).

With the exception of oil, Middle Eastern countries have few goods to offer Cuba. It is not surprising, therefore, that trade between the two has not assumed large proportions (See Tables 2.2 and 2.3). Although trade between Cuba and the Middle Easte has shown signs of expansion since 1959, import and export flows have fluctuated significantly since the 1970s. Furthermore, the poor quality of the data available makes any statement on Cuban-Mid-East trade tentative and any conclusion risky. Insufficient information in Cuban sources, for instance, makes reaching an estimate on trade balance difficult, if not impossible. The main reasons behind this is the statistical gap for 1981-1985 in the *Anuario estadistico*, specifically in regards to imports from countries in the region. Moreover, the data does not include Cuban personnel services abroad (i.e., the export and payment for *internacionalista* white and blue collar workers). In some cases, total salaries paid to Cubans may be higher than traditional commodity trade. The exclusion of such sources of foreign exchange distorts the real picture of the benefits Cuba gains from commercial transactions with Arab countries. Finally, volume of trade might be a misleading indicator of Cuba's economic interest in befriending the Arabs. While at present the quantity of exports and imports is not of vital importance to either side, in the future, Cuba may turn to her Arab friends with the hope of getting special concessions if Moscow ever cuts oil shipments to Havana. The prospect of Arab investment in or loans to Cuba might be as attractive. In June 1981, representatives of the National Bank of Cuba met with Arab bankers in Spain and negotiated a 60 million dollar loan to finance projects in economic and social development.[33]

In spite of the scant data, several trade patterns emerge. First, trade between Cuba and Middle Eastern countries in general experienced a remarkable growth in the 1970-1980 period, exactly at the time when Cuba expanded its role in the region. Second, the trend ended in 1981-1982 with a dramatic downturn which has, for the most part, continued until the mid-1980s.

Table 2.2
Cuba's Exports to Selected Middle Eastern Countries (1958-1985)

(Thousands of Pesos)

Country	1958	1965	1970	1975	1980
Algeria	138	1,162	3,358	22,771	93,435
Arab Republic of Egypt	1	7,207	2,606	5,750	50,084
Iran	398	3,922	---	---	---
Iraq	1,524	7,367	1,341	23,276	113,365
Israel	1,183	536	11	45	98
Lebanon	123	593	976	18,737	1,097
People's Democratic Republic of Yemen (PDRY)	---	---	---	---	---
Saudi Arabia	194	175	309	1,247	2,060
Syria	3,361	3,544	7,240	21,024	41,834

Country	1981	1982	1983	1984	1985
Algeria	103,387	68,460	44,151	11,992	8,172
Arab Republic of Egypt	65,480	42,900	51,040	23,454	22,065
Iran	116	252	10,844	---	---
Iraq	54,956	31,540	25,585	15,628	14,706
Israel	147	38	47	---	0
Lebanon	3,670	12,508	4,611	1,419	2,721
People's Democratic Republic of Yemen (PDRY)	81	46	78	431	2,151
Saudi Arabia	1,701	1,313	7,428	879	2,024
Syria	31,608	23,206	18,459	16,794	7,562

Source: Anuario estadístico de Cuba, 1985, pp. 386-387.

Table 2.3
Cuba's Imports from Selected Middle Eastern Countries (1958-1985)

(Thousands of Pesos)

Country	1958	1965	1970	1975	1980
Algeria	73	2,199	4,263	1,862	479
Arab Republic of Egypt	18	11,095	1,924	1,373	---
Iran	36	---	---	---	---
Iraq	19	---	---	---	---
Israel	86	---	44	---	---
Lebanon				4,606	---
People's Democratic Republic of Yemen (PDRY)	---	---	---	94	---
Saudi Arabia	1	---	---	---	---
Syria	---	---	3,225	338	---

Country	1981	1982	1983	1984	1985
Algeria	550	301	1,088	523	14,816
Arab Republic of Egypt	---	---	---	---	260
Iran	---	---	---	---	---
Iraq	---	---	---	4,029	2,329
Israel	---	---	---	---	---
Lebanon	---	---	---	---	---
People's Democratic Republic of Yemen (PDRY)	---	---	---	---	---
Saudi Arabia	---	---	---	---	---
Syria	---	---	---	---	---

Source: <u>Anuario estadístico de Cuba</u>, 1985, pp. 390-431.

Except for exports to the PDRY and Iran, Cuban exports to her other trading partners in the region have declined sharply. The downward shift might be explained by the economic crisis which has strapped the island and the global economy in the 1980s and the low world prices for the islands' export commodities. For instance, exports to Iraq peaked at 113,365 million pesos in 1980. The following year, Cuban exports to that country did not reach half that amount, totalling 54,956 million pesos. Third, the island's principal Middle Eastern commercial partners in order of importance are Iraq, Algeria, Egypt, and Syria. Except for Egypt, the rest are close political allies of the Cuban government. Two countries which are not close to Havana, Saudi Arabia and Lebanon, also figure as trade partners of relative regional importance. The case of Saudi Arabia is of special interest. Riyadk and Havana have not exchanged diplomatic recognition; their informal relations have been characterized by tension and mutual dislike. Yet, Saudi-Cuban trade has continued, which shows pragmatism on both sides and the divorce of politics from economics.

The Middle East has been of increasing importance to Cuba's international economic relations not only through trade but also through services provided (i.e. construction, health, and other technical assistance). This trend will continue, especially if Moscow pressures Havana to diversify its economy and reduce its dependence on Soviet preferential treatment. The prospect of economic gain is an added incentive for Cuba to pursue closer contacts with the region.

CONCLUSION

Since 1959, Cuba's contact with the Arab world have continuously expanded and have taken a variety of forms. Cuba's Mid-East policy has combined ideology and pragmatism and old and new elements of the island's international relations. The island's involvement has stemmed from Castro's and the Soviet's interests. By the 1980s, Havana was an influential actor in the politics of several Arab countries and groups.

NOTES

1. See, for instance, Luis Gomez Wanguerment, "La crisis del cercano oriente," *Politica Internacional*, Año 6, No. 21, 1968, pp. 43-78.

62

2. Luis Gomez-Wanguerment, "Cronologia del Medio Oriente," *Politica Internacional*, Año 5, No. 18, p. 158.

3. Quoted in Luis Gomez-Wanguemert, "La crisis del cercano oriente," *Politica Internacional*, Año 6, No. 21, 1968, p. 70.

4. Ibid.

5. Raul Roa, "Discurso del Ministro de Relaciones Exteriores, doctor Raul Roa, en la Reunion Ministerial de los Paises no Alineados," *Proyeccion Internacional de la revolucion cubana*, (La Habana: Editorial de Ciencias Sociales, 1975), pp. 403-432.

6. Ibid., p. 430.

7. Zelmys M. Dominguez Cortina and Luis Mesa Delmonte, "Las fuerzas de despliegue rapido y la region del Golfo Arabo Persico," *Enfoque*, 1985, no. 7, pp. 1-70.

8. *Bohemia*, Vol. 75, No. 11, pp. 50-57.

9. This section is based principally on Yoram Shapira, "Cuba and the Arab-Israeli Conflict," in Carmelo Mesa-Lago, ed., *Cuba in the World*, (Pittsburgh: University of Pittsburgh) pp. 153-166.

10. For further discussion see a general work on Cuba's international relations.

11. Shapira, pp. 156-157.

12. K. S. Karol, *Guerrillas in Power*, (London: Jonathan Cape, 1971) p. 400.

13. Shapira, p. 156.

14. H. Michael Erisman, *Cuba's International Relations: The Anatomy of a Nationalistic Foreign Policy* Boulder: Westview 1985 p. 50. On the Nasser-Castro connection see Juan Benemelis, *Cuba's Policy in Africa*, (Unpublished manuscript).

15. See discussion below under *Syria*.

16. Interview with Juan Benemelis, ex-Cuban official, Miami, November 8, 1985.

17. Quoted in Shapira, p. 160.

18. Based on R. Craig Nation, "The Sources of Soviet Involvement in the Middle East: Threat or Opportunity," in Mark V. Kauppi and R. Craig Nation, eds., *The Soviet Union and the Middle East in the 1980s*, (London: Lexington Books, 1983) pp. 56-57.

19. Alvin Z. Rubinstein, "The Soviet Presence in the Arab World," *Current History* 80 (October 1981): 313-314.

20. Ibid., p. 314.

21. Oded Eran, "Soviet Middle East Policy: 1967-1973," in Itamar Rabinovich and Haim Shaked, eds., *From June to October: The Middle East Between 1967 and 1973*, (New Brunswick: Transaction Books, 1978) pp. 38-41.

22. Ibid., p. 40.

23. Ibid., p. 38.

24. Ibid.

25. Erisman, p. 83.
26. Quoted in Ibid., p. 85.
27. Ibid., p. 104.
28. *F.B.I.S. Africa and the Middle East*, 4 April 1976.
29. See Fehmy Saddy, ed., *Arab-Latin American Relations: Energy, Trade, and Investment*, (New Brunswick: Transaction Books 1983).
30. Juan Benemelis, "Cuban Leaders and the Soviet Union" (Paper presented at the Seminar on Soviet-Cuban Relations in the 1980s, University of Miami, November 8, 1985), p. 24.
31. Ibid., p. 20.
32. See Erisman, p. 131.
33. *Cuban Chronology*, 25 June 1981.

3

The Implementation of
Cuban Foreign Policy in the Middle East:
Country by Country

This chapter will examine Cuba's bilateral relations with Middle Eastern countries.

PEOPLE'S DEMOCRATIC REPUBLIC OF YEMEN
(PDRY OR SOUTH YEMEN)

The People's Democratic Republic of Yemen is Cuba's closest ally in the Middle East. Havana's influence on the political and economic life of that nation is far reaching. No other country in the region has received as much Cuban assistance and attention as South Yemen. In no other country has Cuba penetrated the top echelons of the state as deeply as in the PDRY. The reasons are twofold: first, the PDRY's political and economic backwardness has made the country seek external cooperation from sister nations; and, second, Soviet commitment to that country. The history of Cuba-PDRY relations empitomizes the best, as well as the worst, possible scenarios for Cuba's policy in Middle Eastern countries. The benefits Cuba has accrued from its involvement in South Yemen have been limited, and will continue to be limited, by costs arising from the tumultuous nature of South Yemeni politics.

Cuba's military diplomacy in the Middle East started in 1973 when it sent an advisory mission to Aden. Relations between the PDRY and Cuba, however, antedate this mission. Cuba's relations with South Yemen can be traced back to 1966. The first documented contact between Cuban officials and the future leaders of the PDRY occurred during the 1966 Tricontinental Conference in Havana. British occupied South Yemen was represented by members of the National Liberation Front (NLF), one of the two principal groups fighting to end

British colonialism. The conference passed a resolution in support of the NLF and armed struggle in South Yemen. The resolution also called for international aid and solidarity.[1] In November 1972, five years after South Yemen had achieved independence, a Yemeni delegation visited Havana. The visit not only laid the groundwork for the formalization of relations but also reflected the ideological bond between the two nations. Fidel Castro received the visitors, and *Granma* reported that:

> In view of the exemplary position of dignity maintained by the revolution in Democratic Yemen, the Cuban delegation reaffirmed its conviction of the need to consolidate Democratic Yemen as a pillar of the liberation movements on the Arab peninsula and in the rest of the Arab world.[2]

With these words the PDRY was inducted into a special category of Third World states and the revolutionary credentials of its leaders were validated. During the visit, the notion of Cuba as a model for the PDRY emerged. The PDRY and Cuba have continued to stress the historical and ideological ties between both states. They have reaffirmed their commitment to develop strong relations based on "the basic interest of the two countries" and "those of all socialist and progressive" nations.[3]

The 1972 visit was important for another reason. While on the island the South Yemenis requested Cuban aid for Dhofar rebels fighting in Oman. Months later, Cuban assistance was forthcoming. Castro sent 200 advisers to train the PDRY's army and the Dhofar guerrillas. Havana supplied what the Soviets were not willing to furnish directly.[4] Interestingly, the PDRY government criticized Moscow's weak support while it praised Cuba's commitment to the struggle. Cuba's decision surely must have had Soviet blessing. By 1972, the foreign policy differences which had pulled at the Cuban-Soviet partnership had been, for the most part, resolved. It is unlikely that so soon after the 1968 rapprochement, and, given the Middle East's importance to the Soviet Union, Fidel would put Cuba on a course contrary to Soviet interest or not approved by the Kremlin.

Military and security affairs dominated the relations between Cuba and the PDRY during the initial years. In addition to establishing a military mission, the Cubans helped to organize a people's militia and taught Yemeni pilots how to fly Soviet MIGs. As in other countries, Cuban advisers assisted in setting up a neighborhood-based security network similar to the CDRs (Committees for the Defense of the Revolution). Cuban presence in South Yemen peaked (at around 700) by mid-1974. Thereafter, Cuba's massive troop deployment in Angola and

Aden's withering support for the rebels in Oman, caused a reduction in the number of Cubans in the country, levelling off at close to 200.[5] Apparently some of the Cuban personnel was transferred to Angola and, later, Ethiopia. As a result of the emphasis of military relations, the FAR has developed deep reaching contacts within the PDRY leadership and the state bureaucracy.[6] The FAR's intervention on behalf of Abdal-Fattah Ismail during his 1978 coup against Salem Robaya Ali is evidence of the influence of the Cuban military on domestic South Yemeni politics.

Strategically, the PDRY was of value to Cuba during the Angolan and Ethiopian campaigns. Located close to the Horn of Africa, South Yemen provided Cuba with the possibility of transporting soldiers stationed there to Angola and to Ethiopia.[7] Moreover, in terms of regional diplomacy, South Yemen was founding member of the Aden Pact which joins Libya, Ethiopia, and the PDRY in diplomatic and economic cooperation. Like the PDRY, Libya and Ethiopia are close allies of the Cubans. The Aden Pact countries offer the island the opportunity to coordinate policies with its allies.

During the past 10 years, Cuba and the PDRY have signed agreements in a host of fields: education, economy, science, information, and culture. An example of one accord, concluded in 1981, ratified the "scholarship granted by Cuba for the training of [PDRY] youths at higher education schools."[8] The agreement called for the exchange of teaching and bibliographic materials and of delegations of higher and technological education. Additionally, the accord provided "for the exchange of specialists and officials to study the development of the central cultural and scientific life in the two countries."[9]

Economic cooperation agreements have covered a variety of sectors: agriculture (poultry, livestock, seeds, crops); construction (housing, hospitals, schools); light industry; steel; transportation; tourism; and fishing.[10] Allegedly, Cuban technicians have been assisting the PDRY in offshore oil exploration (something which has displeased Saudi Arabia).[11] There have been recent indications that the PDRY has found oil reserves and, therefore, the future of the oil industry is quite promising. Oil would not only provide Aden with a much needed source of income and power, but would benefit Havana as well. Cuba's interest in the PDRY may grow proportionally to the success of the oil exploration.

Hundreds of Cuban workers have offered their services in South Yemen. For instance, members of a construction brigade, led by Ramon Castro Ruz, trained South Yemeni workers in constructing pre-fabricated housing. (On leaving Aden, Ramon Castro Ruz was presented with the Medal of Solidarity by the

Prime Minister, Ali Nasir Muhammed Al-Hasani.) Cuban development assistance to the PDRY has been non-paid due to the poor state of the Yemeni economy. The discovery of oil would change this.[12]

Cuban-PDRY solidarity is based not only on joint military and socio-economic ventures, but on an ideological understanding that is reflected on their relations with Moscow and their position on regional and world issues. An official message from Ali Nasir Muhammed Al-Hasani to the Cubans, on the occassion of Fidel Castro's reelection, stated that:

> We greet the profound positions of principles that have been established by your party on behalf of solidarity with the struggle of our Arab peoples and of support for the people's revolutionary struggle to eliminate the threats of the enemy and the hostility of imperialism. We are convinced that your militant collaboration with our struggle will be increasingly strengthened now and in the future for the purpose of achieving our noble objectives-- the revolutionary example of our parties and our peoples.[13]

The PDRY and Cuba, Communist countries closely aligned with the U.S.S.R., share the view that socialist countries are the vanguard in the Third World's struggle for national liberation.[14] Together they have collaborated with guerrilla groups in the Yemen Arab Republic (YAR or North Yemen) and in Oman. In the Middle East, they both support the Palestinian cause and condemn Israel, Zionism, and the U.S. Cuba and the PDRY have attacked conservative Arab countries. (The PDRY has engaged in border clashes against Saudi Arabia.) In Lebanon, they stand by the Lebanese Communist Party and other "progressive forces." In Central America, they support the Sandinistas and the El Salvadoran guerrillas. In most, if not all, international issues the two countries share a common position.

Ideological affinity has provided room for Yemeni-Cuban collaboration in the creation of a Soviet style political system in the PDRY. Cuba's experience in this area has been of value to the PDRY. The PCC, the FAR, and other party and state organizations have established links with their South Yemen counterparts and have served as consultants in the task of state and nation building. Examples abound. Cubans helped in the establishment of the Yemeni Peoples' Defense Committees. Division General Julio Cesar Regueiro presided over a celebration of the eleventh anniversary of Aden's armed forces held at the FAR headquarters in Havana.[15] In this way, Cuba serves as a model for the PDRY to follow, a blueprint of political and economic Sovietization.

Havana has acted as a lobbyist for Aden's interest in Moscow. According to a former Cuban intelligence officer who worked in the PDRY, Cuba played a "determining role in getting the Kremlin to limit its military aid to North Yemen and reallot it to the client state of South Yemen..."[16] For South Yemen the Cuban lobby in the Soviet Union is of great value, an added incentive to cultivate Cuba's friendship. In turn, the lobbying function demonstrates to the Soviets the Cubans' ability to communicate with other Third World peoples. Consequently, the island's value and usefulness as a channel of communication for Soviet policymakers increases.

Cuba-PDRY relations reveal important dimensions of Cuban-Soviet interaction. Cuba's policy toward third countries is both dependent on and independent from the Soviet Union. The reason is that Cuba functions as a transmission belt. On one hand, Cubans transmit Soivet interests to third countries. On the other, the Cubans can reverse the direction of the belt, sending signals to Moscow which could alter Soviet policy. Therefore, Cuba is both an active and a passive foreign policy agent in the Middle East. While the island follows general Soviet guidelines, it has also used its power to influence Soviet behavior.

Havana's involvement in the PDRY has been successful in spreading Cuban and Soviet influence in that nation and in that area of the globe. Cuba, as a result, has accrued certain benefits from its incursion into South Yemen. However, there have been high risks involved stemming from the fragmented and volatile politics of that country. In no other country of the region or of the world has the island encountered factionalism, personal rivalries, violence, and struggle for power all intertwined as in the PDRY. The nature of Yemeni politics has threatened Cuba's policy there and has raised the issue of factionalism within the Cuban foreign policy apparatus. During the 1978 coup in the PDRY Carlos Rafael Rodriguez and Osmani Cienfuegos, who had been appointed by Castro to be in charge of foreign policy for the Middle Eastern region, supported opposing groups within the PDRY. Cienfuegos backed the moderates while Rodriguez the more pro-Soviet faction.[17]

On several occasions the Cubans in South Yemen have been caught in the crossfire between government leaders, not knowing which side to support or how to end the conflict. This appears to have been the case in the 1986 Civil War, as well as in the 1978 coup against Salem Robaya Ali. In 1986 different branches of the Yemeni Armed forces were divided over whom to support. The air force sided with Ali Nassir Muhammad while the militia and the army split along personal, geographic, and tribal lines.[18] This presented Cuba with a serious dilemma.

Although Cuba's influence in the Yemeni air force is probably stronger than in other branches, Cuba has had contacts with both the army and the militia. Furthermore, the January 1986 events caught the Soviets by surprise and left the Cubans without clear policy directives to follow.

Such scenarios are full of risks and difficult choices for Cuba. First, who should Havana support? What if the Cuban side loses? What if the Soviets and the Cubans disagree over whom to support (as in Angola)? Second, the civilian and military missions in these countries may, as it has been the case in South Yemen, sympathize with different elite factions and may end up supporting contending groups. In such cases, a coherent Cuban policy would be unsustainable. Finally, having to choose between opposing factions abroad may help surface latent factionalism or rivalries within the Cuban foreign policymaking establishment. Factionalism abroad, both in local and regional politics, may heighten factionalism within the Cuban elite.

THE PALESTINE LIBERATION
ORGANIZATION (PLO)

Along with the PDRY, the PLO is Cuba's closest friend in the Middle East. Havana's ties to several PLO factions, and their leaders, provide a source of leverage to mediate internal PLO struggles. Consequently, Cuba is potentially influential in solving inter-Palestinian disputes which would have an impact on peace and war in the region. Castro has realized the potential benefits of a policy of conciliation and has worked backstage to bring the warring PLO factions together. The goal has been elusive, although PLO reunification in early 1987 harbors the possibility of unity. Ideological commonalities and practical benefits for both sides draw Havana and the Palestinian groups together.

Cuba's support for the PLO was manifested at international conferences held in Havana and abroad in the early 1960s.[19] Since then Havana has increasingly supported the PLO at the expense of its relations with Israel. Until 1973, the regime tried to follow the dual paths of recognition of Israel and rhetorical defense of the Palestinian position. The break of relations with Israel in 1973 allowed Cuba to strengthen its ties with the PLO. Cuba granted the PLO full diplomatic status in 1974. The organization established its first embassy-level representation in the Western Hemisphere in Havana that same year.

Support for a Palestinian homeland has been at the heart of Cuba's Middle Eastern policy since the 1960s. Havana considers the Palestinian problem the central issue of the Arab-Israeli crisis and contends that peace in the region is impossible without the establishment of a sovereign Palestinian state.[20] Although Cuba has never denied Israel's right to exist, the island regards the Palestinians as a colonialized people and defends their right to self-determination. From the Cuban perspective, the PLO is the resistance force spearheading the struggle for national liberation.

On a wide range of issues the island and the PLO share a common viewpoint. The PLO and the Cuban government have issued a host of joint communiques regarding the situation in the Middle East. A joint statement released in 1981, after a four day visit by Faruq Qaddumi, PLO Political Department Chief:

> reaffirms Cuba's recognition of the PLO as the only and legitimate representative of the Palestinian people and stresses the Cuban Government's position that the Middle East will never have a just, stable and lasting peace until the rights of these Arab people to self-determination and independence are respected. Both parties also condemn the alliance betwen the United States and Israel against the Arab progressive states and the Camp David agreement and they demand the immediate end to the criminal Zionist attacks on Palestinian refugee camps and Lebanese villages.[21]

The agreement also singled out the contribution of the socialist nations to the struggle of the Arab people while emphasizing "the need to strengthen the unity of action of the non-aligned countries."[22] This juxtaposition of praise for the Socialist bloc and non-alignment is a trademark of Castro's natural ally thesis.

> Characteristic of Cuban policy in the area, the document expresses Cuba's solidarity and support for the efforts made by Algeria, Libya, Syria, the People's Democratic Republic of Yemen and the PLO, members of the Steadfastners [and Confrontation Front] states, to prevent imperialism from carrying out its plans in the Middle East.[23]

The agreement ends ritualistically, both parties pledging "their solidarity with anti-imperialist struggle of the Latin American people."[24]

Non-alignment and support for the "progressive" Arab countries binds the PLO and Cuba. Among other issues, both parties espouse black rule in South Africa, support for the MPLA in Angola and for the Sandinistas in Nicaragua.[25] At the same time, they attack Israel and U.S. regional and global policies. The PLO's closeness to Moscow has opened doors of collaboration with Havana. The PLO-Soviet Union-Cuba triangle has facilitated policy coordination; for instance, on behalf of an international Mid-East peace conference. Cuba and the PLO hold meetings in Havana, throughout the Middle East, and around the world.[26] In February 1984, after Chernenko's funeral, Castro and Yasir Arafat met in Moscow to discuss Middle Eastern affairs.[27] Top PLO officials travel to the island to confer with the Cuban decision-makers, or their Cuban counterparts travel to Tunis or Algiers, especially during crises such as the Israeli invasion of Lebanon.[28]

In the capacity of adviser, and partner, Cuba is intimately linked to the organization. Not only has the island's ambassador to the U.N. sponsored pro-Palestinian resolutions and voiced concern for their cause, Cuba has sponsored several international conferences of solidarity with the Palestinian people. In turn, Arafat has taken the side of Cuba in the Non-Aligned Movement. In other international organizations the PLO and Cuba have chartered a common course of action.

In addition to providing international lobbyist services, Cuba has allegedly trained PLO fighters. Although rumors of Palestinian training camps in Cuba cannot be substantiated, documents captured in the PLO camps by Israel's Defense Forces during the 1982 invasion of Lebanon provide evidence of a guerrilla connection. Among other things, the PLO mission in Havana issued instructions in Spanish on how to sabotage railroad lines, underground cables, and motor vehicles. One document is a letter by a Palestinian student in Cuba. The writer, a medical student, explains that he takes courses in dialectics, political economy, and the world workers movement.[29] The letter reflects the internal divisions within the PLO:

> The Fatah tried through the office of the Liberation Organization to pressure the Cubans not to carry out the celebration [of the 13th Anniversary of the establishment of our Front] and they moved the site of the celebration from the university hall to the International Friendship and Solidarity House. But they did not succeed, we did not invite Fatah to celebrate with us as not to cause problems. Every year they try to disrupt the celebrations.[30]

At least some of the Palestinian students who are educated in Cuba become engaged in PLO guerrilla units upon their return to the Middle East. In 1983 *Bohemia* interviewed a Palestinian doctor who had studied in Cuba and later participated in guerrilla activities.[31] Nevertheless, military training has not been the dominant aspect of Cuba's relations with the PLO. The island has channeled most of its energy in pursuing a policy of Palestinian conciliation.

Strife within the PLO has been of deep concern to the island. Factionalism, on the one hand, reduces the ability of the PLO to exert pressure, negotiate, and get its demands met; on the other, it raises the difficulties and costs for Cuban policy. A united Palestinian and Arab front would increase the chances for success for Cuban and Soviet policy. In 1983 the PCC issued a statement criticizing the armed clashes within the different Palestinian groups. The document stated that:

> our party views with profound concern the continuation of fratricidal fighting among Palestinians in northern Lebanon ... It adds that the struggle within the Palestinian resistance benefits only the Zionists and imperialists, who are observing and encouraging the confrontations ... [32]

The PCC proceded to "issue a call to all parties implicated in the conflict to respect the cease fire and to begin negotiations ... and to again use their weapons against the fundamental enemy--Zionism and imperialism."[33] The "declaration of the Communist Party of Cuba regarding the confrontation at the heart of the Palestinian resistance" lashed out against "those who engage and support the inner struggle," which could be understood as a reference to Syria, and, to a lesser extent, Iran.[34]

Although Cuba has paid lip service to PLO unity since the 1960s, it was not until the 1970s and 1980s that the island commited itself to help bring it about through a policy of mediation. Castro has been in a position to pursue this course for he enjoys good relations with the principal PLO leaders (Yasser Arafat of Al Fatah; George Habah of the Popular Front for the Liberation of Palestine (PFLP); and, Nayib Harvatimah of the Popular Democratic Front for the Liberation of Palestine (PDFLP). In early October 1983, Levi Farah, Cuban Minister for Construction Abroad, held a three day series of meetings in Damascus with the members of opposing Fatah factions. During the mediation process, Farah extended an invitation for the parties involved to meet in Havana:

> An official Palestinian source affirmed here today that Cuba has reiterated its call for the two Fatah factions to meet in the Cuban capital ... He informed them that his country is very concerned about this issue and that it will continue its efforts to end the dispute.[35]

In 1986-1987, Cuba tried once again to bring together the splintered organization. During that period Cuban officials received in Havana representatives from several PLO factions. It is not coincidental that while these meetings were taking place, the PLO leaders moved closer together. In 1987 in Algiers the contending factions hammered out an agreement of unity, putting aside, at least for the time being, personal and ideological rivalries.

Cuba helps the PLO in another important way: as liaison to other Latin American countries, particularly revolutionary states and groups. For example, the PLO has gained access to the Sandinista government in Nicaragua, partly thanks to the Cubans. Managua granted the Palestinians formal diplomatic recognition on July 22, 1980, and the PLO proceeded to open an office in that city. According to Sandinista officials, the ties between the two groups date to the early 1970s:

> There is a long standing blood unity between us and the Palestinian revolution ... many of the units belonging to the Sandinista movement were at Palestinian revolutionary bases in Jordan. In the 1970s Nicaraguan and Palestinian blood was spilled together in Amman and in other places during the Black September battles.[36]

According to the Anti-Defamation League of B'nai B'rith:

> On March 6, 1978 in Havana, Cuba, and the Sandinistas signed a joint communique with the Democratic Front for the Liberation of Palestine [a more extreme constituent member of the PLO] declaring war against Yankee imperialism, the racist regime of Israel and the dictatorship of Anastasio Somoza .. .[37]

Speaking in Havana in July 1980, Arafat declared his support for Nicaragua as an "internal progressive" country and equated Somocismo with Zionism.[38] The mutual support between the PLO and the Sandinistas has been mostly rhetorical. There are a few PLO members in Nicaragua and little PLO aid and investment. What is important in the Cuba-PLO-Nicaraguan connection is the internationalization of both the Middle East and the Central American crises.

Reports allege that Cuba and the PLO have worked together in training Latin American guerrillas in South Yemen, Lebanon, and Libya, and also suggest that they have cooperated in training missions in the Soviet Union, North Africa, and Iraq. These reports connect the PLO and Havana to an international terrorist network.[39] One source claims that the Cuban Embassy in Paris has worked with George Habash of the PFLP and with Black September, another radical PLO faction.[40]

In dealing with the PLO, Cuba has pursued a delicate balance due to the factional nature of the organization. Havana must maintain apparent equidistance between rival groups so as not to lose friends and discredit its policy of conciliation and neutrality. Up to now, the policy has paid off, largely as a result of Castro's charisma, which has enabled him to attract opposing factions and bring them together. Cuba's influence within the PLO would seem to indicate an important backstage role in the internal politics of the organization and, by extension, in regional developments as well. For the Soviets this has been an appealing prospect. For Castro, the possibility of becoming a player in the Arab-Israeli conflict, however small his part might be, has also been an attractive prospect. However, in the Middle Eastern web, Castro has been constrained. He has not been able to move too close to Arafat's PLO without risking his friendship with Syria's President Hafiz Al-Assad.

SYRIAN ARAB REPUBLIC

Syria was one of Cuba's earliest allies in the Middle East, with significant military and social ties between both countries dating back to the mid-1960s. Official diplomatic relations were established in August 1965. Since then, Syria has been a focal point of Cuba's policy in the Middle East. In 1973 Fidel Castro's military commitment to Syria inaugurated a new stage in revolutionary foreign policy, military internationalism. After the mid-1970s, as the island expanded its contacts with other countries and groups in and outside the region, the attention devoted to Syria was diffused. Nevertheless, Cuba-Syrian relations have continued to be warm and cooperative, embracing a variety of fields. Ties to Moscow, as well as broad ideological affinity, have made Havana and Damascus likely partners. Although Syria is not a Marxist-Leninist state, the official ideology of the Syrian regime shares commonalities with both Castroism and practical Marxism-Leninism.

Regional power politics and common foreign policy interests explain, and sustain, Cuban-Syrian relations. According to the Cubans, anti-imperialism has bonded them and the Syrian people. (While Cuba struggles against U.S. imperialism in the Caribbean, Syria must contend with Zionism and U.S. imperialism in the Arab world.) Jesus Montane Oropesa, head of the General Department of Foreign Relations of the Central Committee of the PCC, declared that the Cuban-Syrian friendship was based on Cuba's support of "Syria in its confrontation with imperialism, Zionism and reaction and also

[on] support [of] the Palestinian Arab people in their struggle for self-determination."[41] In reply, Dr. Muhain Bilal, Chairman of the Arab and Foreign Affairs Committee in the Syrian People's Assembly, stated that the Syrian people supported "Cuba's struggle" and condemned "the U.S. threats" against the island.[42]

Mutual interests between Havana and Damascus are, therefore, defined in terms of international issues. Syrian-Cuban joint communiques are illustrative of this:

> Both delegations, after analyzing the situation created by imperialism and zionism in the Middle East, demanded the total withdrawl of the Israeli aggressor force, called for respect for the legitimate national rights of the Arab people of Palestine...
> Both sides support the Paris Agreement and the cease-fire in Vietnam.
> They expressed their support for the struggle of the people and government of the Democratic People's Republic of Korea for the reunification of their country and for the withdrawl of U.S. troops from South Korea. They also expressed their solidarity with peoples of Asia, Africa, and Latin America in their struggle against imperialism...[43]

In addition, Syria and Cuba have coordinated their domestic political and socio-economic positions in the Non-Aligned Movement and other international forums.[44]

Military cooperation has been an important factor in Cuban-Syrian relations. Syria is the only country in the immediate region where Cuban troops have been engaged in actual conflict. The troops were involved in rearguard action against the Israelis in the October 1973 War. During the war, Cubans also provided logistical support, training in the use of Soviet equipment and advice to the Syrians.[45] Between 500 and 700 Cuban tank troops faced front-line action in 1973-1974.[46] *The Economist Foreign Report* reported that:

> The war of attrition began at 5 a.m. on 4 February 1974, when Cuban tank gunners opened up on Israeli positions . .. The hardest bouts of fighting between Israeli and Cubans took place in mid-February, throughout March, in mid-April and mid-May. Throughout the fighting, the Israelis pressed the Americans to make the Russians pull their Cuban legionaires out of Syria.[47]

The article adds that the Israelis noticed an improvement in the quality of the enemy's fighting. However, the Cubans suffered numerous casualties (180 dead, 250 wounded) and their forces had to be relieved by fresh Syrian units. Finally, the surviving Cuban soldiers were airlifted and withdrawn.

> In September, Raul Castro paid a visit to the Cuban units in Syria, accompanied by a team of senior staff officers. The visit lasted a month and involved close supervision of training exercises and the troops' general level of combat-fitness. The end of the tour was celebrated with a festive parade attended by Syria's political and military leaders, during which President Assad and Raul Castro pinned medal on outstanding officers and men of the Cuban force.[48]

In March 1975, most of the Cubans were allegedly flown out in secret to South Yemen and from there to Angola. In 1987, Cuba still maintains a military mission in Syria primarily to train Syrian forces.[49]

The participation of Cuban forces in the Syrian-Israeli war of 1973 reveals salient features of Cuban foreign policy . First, Fidel Castro demonstrated his willingness to commit troops abroad in explosive areas of the world in spite of the risks involved, as long as potential benefits lured him. Second, Syria can be seen as testing grounds for Cuban military internationalism in Angola and Ethiopia. In this light, military involvement in Africa has roots in Cuba's prior conduct. Although the magnitude of the African campaigns were unprecedented. Third, and finally, the spectre of Cuban troop involvement in Middle Eastern conflicts is not as unrealistic as it may seem at first glance.

After 1975, the reduction in Cuban military personnel was compensated by a corresponding increase in Cuban-Syrian economic and cultural cooperation. In the early 1970s Cuban health professionals and medical brigades began to arrive in Syria. Since then, several accords in the economic, technical, cultural, health, and educational fields have been signed. Levi Farah, Minister of Construction Abroad, has visited Syria on several occasions as part of the network of state-to-state cooperation. In the cooperative agreements, Havana supplies the personnel for the projects and Damascus pays for the services they provide. Cooperation has reached the areas of party and legislative relations. The PCC and the National Assembly of the Peoples Power hold consultative meetings with their Syrian counterparts, the Baath Party and the People's Assembly, respectively. The objectives of party and parliamentary exchanges are to coordinate Cuban-Syrian positions international by and to discuss the situation in the Middle East and Latin America.[50]

Syrian delegations visit the island periodically, at least annually since 1980. Cuban delegations also travel to Syria annually. To facilitate these relations, Cuba has established the Cuban-Syrian Joint Inter-Governmental Commission for Economic and Scientific Cooperation, and the Syrians have created the Association for Syrian-Cuban Friendship.[51]

Syria and other Arab countries and groups have acquiesced to, and even welcomed, Cuban involvement in the Middle East, and they have endorsed Cuba's activities on behalf of revolutionary groups elsewhere. In a letter to Fidel Castro on the occasion of the twentieth anniversary of the establishment of diplomatic relations between Syria and Cuba, Al Assad praised the island's important position in the Non-Aligned Movement and among the countries of the Third World "and in its prominent role in the assistance to the struggle for the liberation of the Latin American countries."[52]

In 1980, Damascus' *charge d'affaires* in Havana called relations between both countries "very good" and improving daily.[53] Several issues, however, may get in the way of Syria and Cuba. The main source of tension between the two countries is the PLO. While Castro is in the best of terms with Yasir Arafat, Al Assad is one of Arafat's most powerful enemies. The Syrian head of state is one of the responsible parties for the open, and violent, struggle against Arafat within the PLO. Cuba has responded to PLO infighting with calls for unity and with criticism against those who fan the fires of fraticidal conflict, which could possibly mean Syria. Faced with this sensitive situation, Castro has had to employ his diplomatic dexterity to avoid a rift either with Syria or the PLO.

Cuba has been able to sustain its policy of neutrality and mediation by courting both sides at the same time and avoiding moving closer to one than to the other. In 1986 and 1987 while Havana tried to mediate between PLO factions, Havana cultivated Damascus' goodwill. The Cuban Ministry of Foreign Relations invited the director of the American Department of the Syrian's Foreign Ministry "as part of a program to develop and strengthen relations between Cuba and Syria."[54] Several months before, Castro had sent a message to Al-Assad to express "solidarity with Syria as it faces U.S. and Israeli schemes."[55]

To avoid charges of partisanship in inter-Arab conflicts, Cuba has pursued general, rather than specific, goals. The island's policy is one of the least common denominator, one with which all its Arab allies agree. That is, condemnation of Israel and Zionism, and defense of the Palestinians. Cuba has opted to stress unifying rather than disunifying factors, to reach a minimum consensus of opinion. This modus operandi has safeguarded Havana's capacity to mediate and to act as an agent for inter-Arab unity. The approach explains why Cuba and Syria seemed in total agreement over the Palestinian issue. Under the surface, different perspectives and loyalties threaten to distance both countries if these were brought out into the open.

In the early 1980s, Cuba attempted to mediate the Al Fatah-Syrian dipute. In July 1983 Levi Fatah proposed to Yasser Arafat a meeting to be held in Havana that would bering to the negotiating table representatives of Al Fatah, Syria, the U.S.S.R., and Cuba. Farah's offer, and his Middle East tour at that time, is evidence of Fidel's concern over inter-Arab rivalries and his interest in becoming a power-broker between Arab groups. In June 1983 Fidel sent a message to Syrian President Assad asking him to restrain from any actions which could provoke a confrontation with, and between, the Palestinians. He then launched a shuttle diplomacy effort, headed by Farah. During the month of July 1983 Farah traveled on several occassions between Tunisia, where PLO headquarters are located, and Syria. He met with Palestinian leaders as well as with the Syrian Prime Minister. Although Cuba's mediation had some positive short-term effects, it failed to resolve the Syrian-Al Fatah conflict.

ALGERIA

Fidel Castro highlighted the bond between Cuba and Algeria in a 1972 speech in Algiers,

> ...customs, languages, and geographic distance separate us, but stronger, undestructible ties unite us: the common struggle against colonialism, against imperialist domination worldwide, the effort to achieve that our peoples leave underdevelopment behind in a titanic battle.[56]

His words apply to the entire region as well, for they represent the official reason for Cuba's involvement in the Middle East. The island's introduction to the Arab world took place in Algeria in the early 1960s, which helps explain why the experience shaped Cuba's subsequent regional policy.

Cuba's relations with Algeria began as aid to a national liberation movement, the Algerian independence forces. After independence, the relations developed into traditional state-to-state diplomacy. The Algerians were one of the first recipients of Cuban military and socio-economic assistance. As such, Algeria was the prelude to the island's internationalism in the

Middle East. Since the events of the 1960s, Cuba has used
Algeria as a conduit to expand its contacts among Arab
countries and a source of historical legitimacy for the pursuit of
proletarian internationalism in the region. In short, Algeria is
the oldest, and one of the closest, of Cuba's allies in the region.
In the mid-1980s, relations between the two countries were
excellent.[57]

The doors for cooperation between Cuba and Algeria
were opened in the early 1960s. During those years the Algerian
Front for National Liberation (FNL) and the recently
established regime in Havana had complementary needs. While
the Algerians sought international backing for their war against
the French colonialists, the Cubans wanted opportunities to put
into practice the international dogmas of the Revolution. The
Cuban government had adopted a position of material and
moral support for radical groups throughout Latin America and
the rest of the world. Fidel Castro became the role model and
the mentor for third world revolutionaries. Admiration,
ideological affinity, and the search for assistance drove Ben
Bella, the father of Algerian independence, to Cuba. Ben Bella's
visit resulted in a commitment by the Cubans to send a small
fighting force of 250, under the command of Guevara, to
Algeria. The decision, planted one of the first seeds of military
internationalism and initiated the island in the difficult terrain
of Middle Eastern politics. The policy bore early, but
longlasting, fruit.

The FNL's victory was a success for Cuba as well. Cuba's
solidarity with Algeria served as an example for other groups
and countries. For Castro, Ben Bella, a much admired hero,
became the bridge to other Arab nations. Bella's approval
legitimized and encouraged Cuba's role as defender of
progressive forces in the region.

Algeria has been the transit point for Cuba's assistance to
the Polisario Front (PF). The PF is at war with the government
of Morocco over the establishment of an independent state in
the Sahara. Havana granted diplomatic representation to the
PF and has provided it with socio-economic assistance. Support
for the PF has led to conflict with Morocco, whose government
Cuba regards as anachronistic and reactionary.

Algier's role as interlocutor of Arab concerns and catalyst
for joint Arab actions has provided Havana with a friendly
meeting point. Algeria has served as a gathering place for Cuba
and the PLO, as well as for Cuba and other Arab groups. Cuban
officials frequently stop over in the Algerian capital in route to
other Arab countries. Between May 1984 and July 1985, Cuba's
Foreign Minister travelled to Algeria on three separate
occassions. Other Cuban officials visited the country during
that same period.

Algerians travel to Cuba periodically. Chaddi Bendjedid, Algeria's Prime Minister, was Castro's guest in May 1985. He was met with one of the biggest welcome ceremonies ever organized for a foreign dignitary. In turn, Castro accepted Bendjedid's invitation to visit Algeria on September 1986. Algeria conferred its highest honor, the Athir Medal of the National Merit Order, to Castro during his 1986 trip.

Algerian-Cuban friendship, however, transcends personalism. The governments of both countries share bilateral and international interests. Since 1979 the relations between the two nations have been regulated by a joint intergovernmental commission for economic, scientific, technical, and cultural cooperation. Collaboration in these areas are wide ranging, from agriculture and livestock breeding to health and hydraulic works. The cultural exchange program for 1985-1986 included "art, films, middle education, information, and youth issues and sports."[58]   Since the mid-1980s, both governments have emphasized the need to increase trade with one another.[59] Cuba has exported sugar, coffee, cocoa butter, and cement to Algeria. Algeria has exported phosphates, zinc, cork, and hydrocarbons to the island.

Common positions on many international issues have forged close ties between Algiers and Havana. Both regimes share similar perspective on the Non-Aligned Movement; the NIEO; the foreign debt crisis; disarmament; the weakening of world markets; and, tensions in Latin America, Central America, and the Middle East. While Algeria has sought, and obtained, Cuba's support for its objectives in the Middle East, (condemnation of Morocco's policy regarding the Polisario Front; recognition of the PLO as representative of the Palestinian people; and, an end to the Iran-Iraq War) Cuba convinced Algeria to endorse the island's policies in Central America.

> Algerian Foreign Minister Ahman Taleb Ibrahim said that, in his talks with Cuban authorities, his country agreed to support the Contadora Group's efforts to obtain a negotiated settlement in Central America.[60]

In the mid-1980s a common agenda has brought Cuba and Algeria closer together. The priorities include, at the regional level, the consolidation of PLO unity and the end of factional infighting. Both countries have played important roles in the PLO's reunification process of 1986-1987. At the bilateral level, both countries have expressed interest in expanding commercial and political ties.[61]   There is ample room for future bilateral, regional, and multilateral collaboration.

IRAQ

Cuban-Iraqi relations encompass a wide range of activities: from military and socio-economic cooperation to trade; from domestic and international political collaboration to conflict mediation in the Persian Gulf War. Havana established diplomatic relations with Baghdad in the early 1960s. By 1962, Cuba had a charge d' affaires in the Iraqi capital. Since then, contact between the two nations has flourished. In mid-1976 Cuba established a military mission in Baghdad. However, there are reports that Iraq and Cuba cooperated in guerilla training as early as 1968.[62] In 1976, 150 Cuban military advisers arrived in the Iraqi capital.[63] From that point on, military cooperation has been an important dimension of Cuba's relations with Iraq. According to William J. Durch, Cuban military advisers trained the People's Militia, a politicized para-military organization, helped coordinate special war exercises, and undertook political education in the armed forces. Durch underscores the significance of this work in the domestic Iraqi system:

> ... Cuban assistance to such forces has had as its object the creation or strengthening of the militia as a counterweight to the regular armed forces. Given the fractious nature of Iraqi politics, it is not unreasonable to assume that Cuba is following that pattern in this case.[64]

In addition to military assistance, Havana has contracted with Baghdad to provide various types of socio-economic services, from construction to medicine. In 1979 Cuba signed a housing contract with Iraq totalling 53 million dollars. Cuban construction workers also built 150 kilometers of highway.[65] Cooperation in health services is vast. In March 1984 Dr. Rodrigo Alvarez Cambras, Professor and Director of the Frank Pais Orthopedic Hospital, led a medical delegation to Iraq. The purpose of the visit was to expand bilateral health collaboration.[66] Between 1984 and 1985, the Cuban medical brigade treated over a million patients, performed 1,743 operations, and assisted in 3,700 births.[67] The work of the brigadistas, and Cuba's health service system, has attracted the interest of Iraqi officials. The Iraqi Health Minister attended an international conference held in Havana, "Health for Everyone: 25 Years of Cuban Experience."

Cuba and Iraq have cooperated in the field of computer sciences, transportation, and education. In 1984, the University of Havana and the University of Mosul in Baghdad entered into an exchange agreement.[68] As a result of a visit of the Iraqi Minister by Youth and Sports to the island in June 1980, both governments signed a cooperation accord in the area of sports and recreation.[69] The Minister headed a group of labor, youth, women, peasant, and student leaders for a 10 day visit to Cuba. In theory, Iraq pays Cuba for these services, providing the island not only with an outlet for labor but also much needed foreign exchange. Iraq, however, might not be meeting all its payments due to the expenses associated with the war with Iran.

Political collaboration between both countries is far-reaching. The Iraqis have established ties with the Union of Communist Youth (UJC), the Federation of Cuban Women (FCW), the Central of Cuban Workers (CCW), the CDR's, and the PCC. It is not clear what, if any, political impact this might have on both countries. What is clear, in any case, is that frequent contacts have led to warm relations. Iraq's sympathy for Cuba was manifested in a gift of seven million dollars after Hurricane Frederic hit the island in 1979.

At the international level, Cuba and Iraq have coordinated many of their actions. For instance Iraq co-sponsored Cuba's draft resolution regarding the status of Puerto Rico in the United Nations Decolonization Committee. In the NAM, Cuba and Iraq have been supportive of each other's positions. Preparations for the Seventh Non-Aligned Summit, hosted by Iraq, resulted in close cooperation between Baghdad and Havana. As previous host and leader of the Sixth Summit, Castro was a key person in planning the Baghdad Conference. In August 1982 the Iraqi Minister of Youth, Ahmad Husayn, again travelled to Cuba to deliver a message regarding the Summit from President Hussein to the Cuban Prime Minister. Castro and Carlos Rafael Rodriguez discussed bilateral relations and the Non-Aligned Movement with the Iraqi delegation. After the stop in Havana, the Iraqis continued on their way to Guyana to meet President Linden Forbes Sampson Burnham, then a close friend of the Castro regime.[70]

Iraq's connection to Cuba has paved the way to other Latin American countries. Havana was the site for the meeting between the Assistant Secretary General of the Arab Socialist Baath Party, Shibila Al-'Aysani, and Nicaraguan President Daniel Ortega, during the third PCC congress in February 1986.[71] The joint Iraqi-Cuban UN resolution regarding Puerto Rico is another case in point.

Cuba's leadership of the Non-Aligned Movement and the government's interest in playing a powerful role in Middle Eastern and world affairs led Castro to attempt mediation in the Persian Gulf War. At times acting alone, and at others in conjunction with other Non-Aligned countries (particularly, Yugoslavia and India), Cuba pursued shuttle diplomacy. In search of a solution Cuban officials travelled on several occasions between Havana, Baghdad, and Tehran in late 1980

and early 1981. From 24 September to 9 December 1980, Isidoro
Malmierca made three trips to the region. Malmierca received
direct instructions from Castro and Rodriguez before leaving on
these assignments.[72] Describing Cuba's mediation, official
sources expressed that:

> Cuba thereby undertakes actions aimed at putting an end
> to the current military fighting between two member
> countries of the non-aligned movement which has grave
> consequences for both, for Third World countries, for the
> non-aligned countries movement and for the interests of
> international peace and security.[73]

Cuba, like the Soviets, adopted a cautious attitude in face
of potentially costly dilemma. Iraq, tied to Moscow by a security
treaty, fights Iran with Soviet arms, and possibly with the help
of the Cuban military mission there. Iraqi President Saddam
Hussein's actions against Tehran damages the Kremlin's, and
Castro's, plans for rapprochement with the Ayatollah Khomeini:

> The Kremlin could not support [Hussein] without spoiling
> its hopes for better relations with Iran, nor could it
> oppose him without weakening what remained of the
> Soviet position in Iraq and losing influence in other Arab
> countries.[74]

The Soviet's safest option has been to remain neutral and to
hope for an end to hostility.
Cuba confronts a similar disjuncture but risks fewer costs
in case of policy failure. While trying to safeguard its bonds
with Baghdad, it has attempted to develop a relationship with
Tehran since 1979. Neutrality was a wise course to adopt;
mediation was wiser. Mediation served the interests of all
parties concerned -- Iran, Iraq, Cuba, U.S.S.R., and the regional
and global communities.
Mediation, however, was not an easy policy to implement.
Clearly, reaching a settlement was even more difficult, and
eventually, elusive. Yet, Cuba juggled its interests and policies
carefully not to upset its relationships with any of the other
states involved in the conflict. Given sufficient diplomatic *savoir
faire*, mediation posed fewer risks and greater benefits than any
other course of action. On Havana's diplomatic offensive
Erisman writes:

> Throughout this process Cuba was careful to consult fully
> with its non-aligned colleagues and to follow their
> instructions precisely so that its critics could not accuse it
> of ideological partisanships, thus demonstrating that the

fidelistas had opted for a leadership style characterized by pragmatic consensus building rather than charismatic radicalism.[75]

This leadership style fits well with the Soviets' cautious moves in the area, especially since the latter's foray into Afghanistan. In this situation, the Cubans were not ideologically partisan, not because of pressure from the Non-Aligned Movement necessarily, but because partisanship undermines Soviet, as well as Cuban, interests in the Persian Gulf.

The hallmark of Cuban foreign policy in the Middle East was evident in Castro's shuttle diplomacy in the Persian Gulf War. First, Cuban-Soviet interests converged. Second, the modus operandi was pragmatic and moderate. Third, diplomatic mediation was the means to reach the end of Cuba's policy.

Cuba's shuttle diplomacy peaked in late 1980; being downgraded thereafter. Although the policy failed, Havana's prestige did not suffer. On the contrary, it might have been enhanced by the leadership demonstrated. Since 1981, Cuba has continued to pursue mediation in less publicized and less dramatic ways. In case that someday Iraq and Iran decide to meet at the negotiating table, Cuba would be a likely candidate for the role of mediator.

IRAN

Cuba's relations with Iran reflect ideological flexibility and the neutrality vis-a-vis inter-Arab conflict, two features of the island's policy in that region of the world. Post-1979 Tehran provided Havana the opportunity to continue expanding the island's contacts in the area and to increase its leverage to mediate the Persian Gulf War. For Iran, Cuba represented an anti-American lobbyist in international organizations; an anti-Zionist sympathizer; and, a useful link to potential sources of support in Latin America.

Relations between Cuba and Iran antedate the Iranian Revolution of 1979. As part of the program to develop the island's ties with Middle Eastern countries, Cuba established diplomatic relations with the Shah's government in 1975. State to state diplomacy, however, was short lived. Havana's dual track policy of combining recognition of the Shah's government with support for anti-regime groups was unacceptable to Tehran. Fourteen months after officially announcing that the two nations had agreed to exchange ambassadors, Iran broke relations with Cuba (7 April 1976). The reason for the rupture was a meeting held a month before between Fidel Castro and the First Secretary of the Iranian People's Party (IPP), a communist organization which adovocated revolution. In 1979 when Ayatollah Khomeini, a strong anti-Communist, reached power, Cuba abandoned its support of the IPP and, in turn, endorsed the Iranian revolution. Interestingly, while Marxism-Leninism was cast aside in favor of pragmatism and flexibility, the tenets of Castroism proved to be the litmus test to determine Cuba's support for revolutionary states.

Fidel has defended the Islamic Revolution since 1979. He has praised it, stating that a real people's struggle was taking place in Iran which exhibited extraordinary force, and he "called on the Cuban people to support and express their solidarity with the struggle of the Iranian people."[76] In an 1979 interview with *Time* magazine, Fidel commented that the Iranian revolution enjoyed enormous popular force and that it would probably "cling to its strong religious and nationalist accent."[77] When asked if he was disturbed by the anti-Marxist views expressed by Ayatollah Khomeini and his followers, the Cuban leader stated that:

> I am not much disturbed. If the revolution can improve the future of the people, it does not matter whether it is based on a Marxist philosophy or a religious philosophy. I know that the Marxists in Iran are supporting Khomeini.[78]

In response to the question, do you think the Marxists will inherit the revolution, Fidel answered that:

> It does not seem likely. And I do not think that it is in their minds. But look, we do not think that there is contradiction between religion and revolution. I have said that Marxists and Christians can be strategic allies.[79]

These statements underscore the relevance of Castroism as the ideological bases of Cuban foreign policy. Anti-Americanism, nationalism, and social change through revolution are basic features of the Iranian situation since 1979. Cuban support for the Khomeini regimes stems from here.

Castro's interest in religion (specifically, liberation theology) as a revolutionary force in Latin America fits well with his perception of Islamic fundamentalism as an agent of social change in the Middle East. During a meeting with an Iranian parliamentary delegation visiting the island in 1981, Castro emphasized the revolutionary role of Islam and said that it should be spread to other Arab masses.[80] On that occassion, Castro also remarked that "he would like to meet the Imam [meaning the Ayatollah]."[81] Interestingly, the Cuban leader has expressed a similar interest in regards to the Pope, which would seem to indicate another attempt to bring religion and Marxism together.

Soon after the triumph of the Khomeini revolution, Havana expressed its willingness to embrace Tehran. In early August 1979 an official Cuban delegation visited the Iranian capital, signalling Cuba's decision to reopen diplomatic relations. Later that month, the Iranian Foreign Minister travelled to Havana. Thereafter, the ties between the two countries grew. The initial steps were characterized by cordial exchanges of governmental delegations. The visits usually ended with anti-U.S. pronouncements. The initial contacts lead to collaboration in the Non-Algined Movement and in other international forums. In 1980 and early 1981, Cuba attempted to seek a mediated solution to the Iran-Iraq War.

Havana's longstanding friendship with Bahgdad was an obstacle to Castro's attempt at mediation. To soothe Iranian fears of partisanship, during 1979 and 1980 Cuba pursued a host of policies in support of the Ayatollah's regime. For instance, the island endorsed Iran's campaign against the U.S.[82] In the NAM, Cuba's solidarity with Iran was evident in the appointment of a Cuban to the position of Latin American vice-president of a conference held in Tehran in June 1980 to investigate U.S. aggression against Iran.

Isidoro Malmierca was Castro's chief envoy in the mediation process begun in 1980. Public sources confirm that Malmierca travelled to Iran on at least three occassions during a one year period. (May and October 1980, and May 1981). The island worked closely with the NAM during this period. By May 1981 the NAM had named a commission to find a solution to the war. In addition to Cuba, the commission included India, the PLO, and Zambia.[83]

The failure of Castro's mediation diplomacy in no way damaged Iranian-Cuban relations. In fact, contacts have continued to expand since the early 1980s. In 1981 during the visit of Iranian parliamentarians Fidel stressed the need to increase ties between Tehran and Havana and added that it was "necessary for the Islamic Republic of Iran to have an embassy in Cuba."[84] The second official Iranian delegation to tour the island was headed by Deputy Foriegn Minister Ahmad Azizi in August 1982. The purpose of the meeting with Castro was to discuss non-aligned matters, including the summit conference, and the strengthening of bilateral relations.[85] From 1984 to 1987, Cuban and Iranian top level delegations have visited each other's countries. The purpose of the visits have revolved around the coordination of common positions in international organizations and the expansion of Cuban-Iranian ties. In 1984, the Iranian President sent a special envoy to Havana to discuss "the proposed plan of the Islamic republic of Iran based on the

expulsion of the Zionist regime from the United Nations."[86]
Fidel Castro expressed support for the proposal and promised to
"exert all our efforts for the implementation of this plan."[87]

Iran is interested in Cuba's friendship. In some ways
Cuba is an attractive ally. Not only is Havana willing to
mediate the Gulf War, it is also able to lobby for Iran in the
U.N. and in the NAM. President Castro, Iranian President
Khomeini and Libyan leader Qaddafi met during the
preparatory session for the Eight Non-Aligned Summit to
discuss a resolution against state terrorism by the U.S.[88] Cuba
can also serve as a middleman between Iran and other Latin
American countries, whose support Iran would like. In a
specific case, Tehran tried to convince Havana to seek votes in
Central America for the anti-Zionist and anti-Israeli resolution
that Iran was to present in the U.N.[89] Cuba has also functioned
as a bridge between Iran and Nicaragua. Iranian officials on
their way to Managua usually stop in Havana. Finally, Cuba
could serve as a mediator between the Soviets and the Iranians,
if the need ever arises.

These points of common interest and mutual benefit must
be tempered by the fact that it took Tehran 5 years (from 1979
to 1984) to open an embassy in Havana. Moreover, in spite of
the fact that the revolutions of both countries exhibited an anti-
American bias, the essence of the Islamic and the Castroite
revolutions are at odds. Iranian mistrust of the Soviets and
rejection of Marxism make relations with Cuba, although
valuable in some ways, troublesome in others. Cuba is
indubitably a Marxist state and has coordinated its foreign
policy closely with Moscow since 1977. (It is unlikely that the
Khomeini regime has forgotten Cuba's contact with the Marxist
IPP in the 1970s). This is enough to serve as a source of
apprehension for Tehran. In addition, Iran's current number
one enemy, Iraq, has been one of Cuba's strongest allies in the
region since the 1970s. As relations with Iran mature, Havana
must be careful not to duplicate the Somalian-Ethiopian
situation. Cuba must maintain a delicate balance between both
sides of the Persian Gulf War. Otherwise, Castro's policy of
neutrality, pragmatism, mediation, and role expansion would be
at risk.

RELATIONS WITH OTHER COUNTRIES

Egypt

The history of Havana's diplomacy toward Cairo can be
divided into three periods: first, the Nasser period (1959-1970);

second, the Sadat period (1970-1980); and third, the Mubarak period (1980-present). Relations between both nations have had an on and off character from one period to the next. Cuban-Egyptian relations have combined ideological and pragmatic concerns.

Havana's relations with Cairo up to 1970 were warm, although Nasser was opposed to Castro's incursion into the region.[90] Castro's anti-Americanism as well as his interest in international support for the Revolution attracted him to Gamal Abdel Nasser, a pan-Arabist and a prominent Third World statesman who had stood up to the U.S. involvement in the Middle East. In an attempt to get Nasser's, and the Arab's, blessing for his global pursuits, Fidel courted the Egyptian leader. In the 1967 Israeli-Egyptian war, Cuba sided with Egypt and offered its assistance. In a May 1967 letter to Nasser, Osvaldo Dorticos, then President of Cuba, wrote:

> It is my pleasure to reiterate to you the militant support and the revolutionary solidarity of the Cuban people with the Arab peoples in their determination to combat the maneuvers, prvocations, threats and aggressions of Yankee imperialism in the Middle East.[91]

But Nasser was not receptive to Castro's overture, for fear of a rival in the leadership of the Third World movement, out of Pan-Arabist conviction, and-or in opposition to increase Soviet influence in the area.

Egypt's break with the Soviet Union in 1972 distanced Havana from Cairo. Antagonism toward Anwar Sadat and his separate peace treaty with Israel (the Camp David Accord) became a cornerstone of Cuban policy in the Middle East. From Havana's perspective, Cairo had sold out to U.S. imperialism and Sadat had betrayed his Arab brothers. Consequently, the Camp David Accords were destined to fail for they did not address the Palestinian issue and did not provide a multilaterally negotiated settlement to the Arab-Israeli conflict. This position was shared with the radical Arab states and the Soviet Union

Neither the fierce condemnation of the Camp David Accords nor the flurry of rhetorical attacks against Sadat led to the severance of diplomatic relations between Cuba and Egypt. Havana's posture was shaped by two sorts of considerations: ideological and practical. The Accords, signed under the tutelage of the U.S., as well as the reorientation of Egyptian foreign policy away from the U.S.S.R., were ideologically unsavory for the Cubans. Havana's position, however, was moderate and pragmatic in comparison to that of Cuba's friends, the radical Arab states. While Havana could gain points with its allies for opposing Cairo's unilateral agreement, it had a lot to lose from cutting relations or from joining the ranks of those Arab nations calling for the expulsion of Egypt from the NAM. By pursuing such a course, the island would foreclose the possibility of future influence over Egypt and would jeopardize valuable commercial transactions. Cuba would also undermine its self-assumed role of inter-Arab mediator. The Cubans exercized their mediating skills at the 1979 NAM meeting in Havana where the issue of the expulsion of Egypt threatened to divide the movement and the Arab states themselves.

Post-Sadat relations with Egypt remain cool, although less strained, as a trip in 1983 by Melba Hernandez, the Cuban Secretary General of the Afro-Asian-Latin American Peoples' Solidarity Organization (AALAPSO or OSPAAL) showed.[92] The Soviets' interest in a rapprochement with the Egyptians, combined with President Mubarak's foreign policy moderation as compared to Sadat's pro-U.S. course, may be the groundwork for a Cuban-Egyptian reencounter.

Jordan

In 1979, at the zenith of Cuba's influence in the Non-Aligned Movement, Fidel Castro met with King Hussein of Jordan. By the time their encounter ended, the two heads of states agreed to establish relations between their respective countries. The 1979 meeting was the culmination of Cuba's attempt to strengthen its ties with Jordan. The objective behind Fidel's initiative was to validate Cuba's policy of reconciliation and unity within the Arab countries. Cuba, in its attempt to play the role of diplomatic middleman, had to forge ties with conservative Arab states such as Jordan.

The designation of a non-resident ambassador to Jordan (usually the Cuban ambassador to Iraq) signalled the reversal of the island's policy toward the Kingdom. Cuba had considered King Hussein a reactionary monarch, a puppet of the U.S. and of Israel, and responsible for the assassination of thousands of Palestinians. Up to 1979, the Cuban press consistently depicted Hussein in the worst terms possible, charging him with a variety of offenses from disloyalty to family members (for reasons of personal power) to selling out his Arab brothers for U.S. economic and military assistance.[93]

Despite the 1979 rapprochement, Cuba continues to regard Hussein critically due to Hussein's conservative policies and his friendship with the U.S. As in the cases of other conservative Arab states (Kuwait, Lebanon, and North Yemen) official diplomatic recognition has not resulted in any significant expansion of contacts. There are several possible explanations for this. First, the receiving country, in this case, Jordan, distrusts the Cubans and prefers not to have them as close partners. Second, the Cubans might have little to offer the Jordanians. Third, the ideological barriers might be too high to be easily surmountable. Finally, Cuba's overture may not ring true to King Hussein. Therefore, it is unlikely that Havana will be able to upgrade its relations with Jordan in the near future.

Kuwait

Ties with Kuwait were established in 1973. In 1982, Kuwait and Cuba agreed to upgrade relations to the level of embassy and to exchange ambassadors. With the exception of a 1983 agreement to exchange radio and television techniques, the ties between both countries have remained weak.[94] A Cuban source states that there are Cuban international workers in Kuwait.[95] It is unlikely that the relationship will change dramatically, for Kuwait does not seem to be interested in expanding relations with Cuba.

Lebanon

The most striking aspect of Cuba's policy toward Lebanon is its duality. The island has maintained traditional state-to-state relations with the country since 1959. Havana, however, has emphasized support for anti-status quo groups and the PLO, rather than support to the Lebanese government.

Cuba has criticized the Lebanese state for being capitalist, rightist, and bourgeoisie. Havana claims that Beirut has collaborated with reactionary Arab forces who serve U.S. interests in the region and whose main purpose is to eliminate the Palestinian resistance.[96] At the same time, the Cubans have defended Lebanese nationalism against Israeli attacks, and have pictured the country as a beseiged victim of Zionism. Cuba has also denounced the massacre of Palestinians and Lebanese citizens throughout the years.

Following the Israeli invasion of Lebanon, in 1982, Cuba seized the occasion to condemn both Israel and the United States. The Cuban Foreign Ministry issued a U.N. resolution denouncing Zionist aggression. A press statement criticized "the acts of genocide the Israeli occupation troops are carrying out against the people of southern Lebanon," and the support of the Zionist government by the United States. The Cuban Foreign Ministry further warned "of the urgent need to halt the detestable Zionist massacring of the Lebanese people."[97]

Official relations between the two countries had been limited to an exchange of ambassadors and other manifestations of formal diplomatic ties. Contrary to Cuba's usual practice with radical counterparts, however, Lebanese government officials have not traveled to Cuba nor have top Cuban leaders been invited on official visits to Lebanon. Neither have joint socio-economic agreements been signed. No Cuban brigadistas have been reported working in Lebanon. Relations are cool, but cordial.

The PLO and the Palestinians have been a central concern of Cuba's relations with Lebanon. Documents captured by the Israelis from PLO headquarters suggested that the Cuban Embassy in Beirut functioned as an important focal point to coordinate Cuban support for the PLO. Aware of such ties, the Israeli military, during its occupation of West Beirut, at one point surrounded the Cuban Embassy with soldiers. Cuba protested vigorously, both in the United Nations and to the Lebanese government, charging that an Israeli general had not only entered the Embassy building (which doubles as residence for the Cuban ambassador) without permission but had also encircled the building with "more than 100 soldiers."[98]

Cuba maintains strong bonds with the Lebanese Communist Party (LCP), and other radical Lebanese political organizations such as the Lebanese National Movement. The LCP has a permanent representative in Havana and LCP officials have traveled to the island. In 1984 Fidel Castro met with some of them. At the end of their visit, LCP Secretary General, George Haivi, delcared that Fidel Castro, "closely follows the events in Lebanon," and shows a "responsible interest" in what occurs there.[99] Haivi added that there was a link between the struggle in Lebanon "and those being waged in Cuba, Central America, and the Caribbean."[100] Cuban support for the LCP, so far as can be documented, appears to be mostly rhetorical: moral support, lobbying, advising. It is possible that more substantial assistance, particularly financial or military, may be provided by the Soviet Union.

Oman and Bahrain

Cuba's commitment to national liberation movements has been manifested in the Middle East. In addition to the PLO, Havana has recognized and offered assistance to groups fighting in Oman and Bahrain.

The most publicized case is that of Oman. Cuba's support to the Popular Front for the Liberation of Oman (PFLO) dates back to the 1960s. The PFLO, a pro-Soviet Marxist guerrilla group, launched a campaign against British colonialism in 1965. By the early 1970s, the rebels controlled parts of the Dhofar region. Cuba, through South Yemen, gave military assitance to the PFLO during this period. In 1973, Iran with the blessing of the U.S. and England, deployed troops and crushed the rebel forces. However, the PFLO did not disappear. Cuban and Soviet continued support to the organization was evident in a February 1985 article in *Granma*.[101]

A less well-known example of Cuban backing of the National Liberation Front of Bahrain (NLFB).[102] Information on the Cuban-NLFB connection is not to be found in the public record. What is available is Cuba's reason for backing the organization. The region is of great economic and strategic importance for both superpowers, but especially for the U.S. due to the fact that around fifty percent of the oil consumed in the Western world is shipped through the Strait of Hormuz. Ideology and pragmatism induce Cuba to support the NFLB. However, the quality and quantity of Cuban support for the organization, if any at all, is not known.

Saudi Arabia

In Cuba's manicheistic worldview, Saudi Arabia falls in the category of reactionary Arab regime. The Cubans, have been critical of the Saudi's domestic and foreign policies, especially their ties to Washington and Saudi funding of the contras in Nicaragua. Havana does not have official diplomatic relations with Riyadh, although Cuba exports reach the Saudi kingdom.

The Saudi-Cuban relationship has been conflictive. Once source of conflict is that the ideologies of both regimes are at odds. Another one is Cuba's involvement in the politics of the PDRY, Saudi Arabia's Marxist neighbor. The Saudi's fear the possibility of Cubans directly, or indirectly, participating in Yemeni-Saudi border clashes, as well as support for internal subversion in Saudi Arabia. In addition, Saudi Arabia has protested South Yemen's oil exploration (in which the Cubans are aiding) claiming that the Yemenis' are tapping Saudi oil.[103]

Another cause of tension between Havana and Riyadh has been the former's assistance to the rebels of the Dhofar region in Oman. The Saudi's feel that the spread of Marxism and Soviet influence in the region represents a threat to their own political system.[104] Finally, the Saudi's, traditional intermediaries of inter-Arab conflicts, may regard the Cubans as competitors in the arena of diplomatic mediation.

Yemen Arab Republic (North Yemen)

In May 1983 Cuba announced the appointment of Jorge Morente Caballero to serve as ambassador to both Kuwait and

94

the Yemen Arab Republic (YAR or North Yemen).[105] The announcement signalled the culmination of a process of rapprochement which started in 1982. That year Cuba and North Yemen signed a cooperation protocol in the fields of fishing, construction, trade, agriculture, education, tourism, and social services. There has been no significant activities between both countries since that time, except for the replacement of Morente Caballero by Julio Imperatorio Grave de Peralta in 1985.[106] Apparently, Cuba has reached a *modus vivendi* with the YAR but relations are cool.

Cuba's 1982 overtures to conservative states such as North Yemen and Kuwait were part and parcel of the island's regional approach. By expanding its influence in all Arab quarters, Cuba would be placing itself in a good position to mediate intra-Arab conflicts and to play a larger role in the region. Havana would not be viewed solely as an ally of the most radical Arab states but as a moderate partner who extended its friendship to any Arab nation willing to respond.

CONCLUSION

Cuba's relations with Middle Eastern countries share basic features in common while also offering points of contrast from one country to another. This points to Havana's pragmatic and flexible approach to the area. However, Cuba's bilateral relations with the Arab nations have sustained the principles of Castroism and have upheld Soviet regional interests. Although benefits have been accrued, the risks associated with involvement in the region are high. The Libyan case (see Chapter 4) illustrates this in detail.

NOTES

1. *Politica Internacional*, Vol. 4, No. 3, 1966, pp. 140-141.
2. *Granma Weekly Review*, 19 November 1972, p. 4.
3. *Granma Weekly Review*, 27 March 1977, p. 3.
4. William J. Durch, "The Cuban Military in Africa and the Middle East: From Algeria to Angola," *Studies in Comparative Communism*, XI (Spring-Summer 1978): 52.
5. Ibid.
6. Interview with Juan Benemelis, Miami, November 8, 1985.
7. See Durch.

8. FBIS Latin America, 20 March 1981, Q. 5.

9. Ibid.

10. FBIS Latin America, 20 June 1980, Q. 2.

11. Interview with Juan Benemelis, Miami, November 8, 1985.

12. Havana Domestic Service in Spanish, 24 June 1983.

13. FBIS Latin America, 2 September 1981, Q. 4.

14. Ibid.

15. FBIS Latin America, 2 September 1981, Q. 2.

16. Ibid., p. 20.

17. Juan Benemelis, "Cuban Leaders and the Soviet Union" (Paper presented at the Seminar on Soviet-Cuban Relations in the 1980s, University of Miami, November 8, 1985), p. 24.

18. Fred Halliday, "Catastrophe in South Yemen: A Preliminary Assessment," *Middle East Report*, March-April 86, No. 16, pp. 37-39.

19. Shapira, pp. 154-156.

20. See for instance, *Granma*, 23 November 1985, p.4.

21. FBIS Latin America, 15 October 1981, Q. 4.

22. Ibid.

23. Ibid.

24. Ibid.

25. FBIS Latin America, 25 July 1980, Q. 1 and 25 October 1981, Q. 4.

26. See for instance FBIS Latin America, 6 September 1983.

27. FBIS Latin America, 17 February 1984, Q. 1.

28. FBIS Latin America, 6 October 1981.

29. "Relations between the Palestinian Terrorists and Cuba" (mimeo) p. 35.

30. Ibid.

31. "Ida sin vuelta," *Bohemia*, Vol. 75, No. 26, 1-07-1983, pp. 76-77.

32. FBIS Latin America, 28 November 1983, Q. 4.

33. Ibid.

34. Ibid.

35. FBIS Latin America, 4 October 1983, Q. 3.

36. Quoted in U.S. Department of State, "The Sandinistas and the Middle Eastern Radicals," (Washington: August 1985), p. 2.

37. Anti-Defamation League of B'Nai B'Rith, "P.L.O. Activities in Latin America," *International Report: Latin America* (May 1982), p. 8.

38. FBIS Latin America, 25 July 1980, Q. 1.

39. See for instance the Anti-Defamation League "P.L.O. Activities in Latin America."

40. Interview with Juan Benemelis, Miami, November 8, 1985.

96

40. Interview with Juan Benemelis, Miami, November 8, 1985.

41. FBIS Latin America, 14 January, Q4.

42. Ibid.

43. *Granma Weekly Review*, 16 June 1974, p. 3.

44. *Granma*, 12 August 1985, p. 3.

45. See Jorge I. Dominguez, "The Armed Forces and Foreign Relations," in Carmelo Mesa-Lago, ed., *Cuba in the World*, Pittsburgh: University of Pittsburgh Press, pp. 46. Durch, pp. 53-54.

46. Durch, pp. 53-54.

47. *The Economist Foreign Report,* "Castro's First Middle East Adventure: Part II, 15 March 1978, p. 6.

48. Ibid.

49. Erisman, p. 49.

50. *Syrie et Monde Arabe*, Vol. 28, No. 343, August 1982, p. 78.

51. *JPRS Latin America*, 18 March 1985, p. 146.

52. *Granma*, Vol. 21, No. 194, 17 August 1985, p. 6.

53. FBIS Latin America, April 20, 1981, Q15.

54. FBIS Latin America, 14 October 1986, Q2.

55. FBIS Latin America, 5 June 1986, Q1.

56. "Fidel Castro, Una amistad que nacio en la comunidad del heroismo," *El Tercer Mundo y el futuro de la humanidad*, p. 57.

57. FBIS Latin America, 22 May 1984, Q6.

58. *Granma*, Vol. 21, No. 131, 19 August 1985, p. 2.

59. FBIS Latin America, 19 June 1985, Q2.

60. FBIS Latin America, 14 May 1985, Q2-3.

61. FBIS Latin America, 20 March 1984, Q4.

62. White House Office of Media Relations, "The PLO in Central America" in *White House Digest*, July 29, 1983, p. 2.

63. Quoted in Durch, p. 56 from *The Economist Foreign Report*, August 1976.

64. Durch, p. 56.

65. *Prisma Latinoamericano*, March 3, 1983, p. 26.

66. FBIS Latin America, March 23, 1984, Q1.

67. *Granma*, Vol. 21, No. 279, 26 November 1985, p.7.

68. *Granma*, Vol. 20, No. 219, 17 October 1984, p. 4.

69. FBIS Latin America, 20 June, 1980, Q3.

70. FBIS Latin America, 11 August, 1982, Q1.

71. FBIS Latin America, 11 February 1986, Q10.

72. FBIS Latin America, 25 September, 1980, Q1.

73. FBIS Latin America, 24 September, 1980, Q1.

74. John C. Campbell, "Soviet Policy in the Middle East," *Current History* (January 1981): 4.

75. Erisman, p. 131.

76. FBIS Latin America, 16 May 1980, Q7.

77. "An Interview with Fidel Castro," *Time*, 4 February 1980, p. 48.

78. Ibid.

79. Ibid.

80. FBIS Latin America, 24 September 1981, Q2.

81. Ibid.

82. Ibid.

83. FBIS Latin America, 4 June 1980, Q3.

84. FBIS Latin America, 14 October 1983, Q4.

85. FBIS Latin America, 16 August 1982, Q2.

86. FBIS Latin America, 1 October 1984, Q1.

87. Ibid.

88. FBIS Latin America, 3 September 1986, Q1.

89. FBIS Latin America, 10 October 1984, Q1.

90. Interview with Juan Benemelis, Miami, November 8, 1985.

91. *Politica Internacional*, 2ndo Trimestre, 1967, p. 297.

92. FBIS Latin America, 14 October 1983, Q4.

93. See, for example "Jordania, servicios pagados," *Bohemia* 64 (14), 7 April 1972, pp. 79-80.

94. FBIS Latin America, 14 October 1983, Q4.

95. *Colaboracion*, No. 2, Abril-June, 1986, p. 5.

96. See "Jordanizacion de el Libano," *Bohemia*, 64 (26): 75-76, 30 June 1972.

97. FBIS Latin America, 7 March 1985, Q1.

98. FBIS Latin America, 21 September 1982, Q1.

99. FBIS Latin America, 12 March 1984, Q7.

100. Ibid.

101. *Granma*, Vol. 21, No. 51, February 1985, p. 5.

102. See Dominguez, Cortina, and Mesa Delmonte.

103. Interview with Juan Benemelis, Miami, November 8, 1985.

104. Ibid.

105. Havana Domestic Service, 6 May 1983.

106. JPRS Latin America, 26 March 1985, p. 35.

4

Cuban-Libyan Relations: A Case Study

One could say that Cuban-Libyan relations were meant to be. The tenets of both countries domestic and foreign policies are remarkably similar.[1] First, the principal thrust of Cuban and Libyan foreign pursuits is the survival, if not the strengthening, of their respective national revolutions of 1959 and 1969. Second, the top leadership of both states seek to expand personal international prestige and aggrandizement of influence abroad; in other words: the internationalization of charisma and whatever resulting power this conveys. Third, Fidel Castro and Muammar Qaddafi espouse variations of the same worldview: nationalism and internationalism (be it proletariat internationalism or pan-Arabism). Fourth, both revolutionary regimes have always reflected a profound anti-Westernism or anti-Americanism (the U.S. being the main target of attacks against imperialism and capitalism). Fifth, both the Cuban and Libyan revolutions inaugurated "egalitarian" social systems at home and have demanded an egalitarian world system abroad via the New International Economic Order. Sixth, both countries adopted a self-image of defender of oppressed peoples of Asia, Africa, and Latin America and, in so doing, have backed "movements of national liberation," "progressive regimes," and "anti-status quo factions." Finally, Cuba and Libya have tried to accomplish the above goals within the framework of non-alignment, although, in different degrees, both have leaned toward the Soviet Union.[2]

The Cuban and the Libyan systems, and their behavior in the international arena, however, are distinguishable from one an other. Broad commonalities have facilitated cooperation of the two states in global activities in the past decade. Although Cuba and Libya share an affinity in general foreign policy goals and tactics at present, it would be a mistake not to realize that friction and even overt hostility have occasionally marred relations at times in the past. A major source of real and potential problems has been, and continues to be, the Soviet Union, with whom the two countries hold different relationships. The revolutionary tendencies of the Caribbean island and the North African country, at times, have results quite dissimilar, especially so if Qaddafi's Islamic fundamentalism is taken into consideration. Nevertheless, the comparison between Libya and Cuba reveals two small countries (in terms of size in the Cuban case and of population in the Libyan) that have leaders with global aspirations. Critics have remarked that Cuba is undersized for Castro's international aspirations; the same can be said of Qaddafi in the Libyan context with equal validity.

OBJECTIVES OF CUBAN AND LIBYAN FOREIGN POLICY

Castro and Qaddafi's revolutionary internationalism has lead them to become interested in lands remote from their own shores as well as in their own region. What specific policy objectives do Cuba and Libya share in the Middle East and Latin America in particular?

In the Middle East, both states dream of shaking the balance of power to the detriment of Israel and the United States. As a corollary, they support the PLO and the creation of a Palestinian state. The means to accomplish the end are basically the same: support of the most radical regional actors. Qaddafi and Castro have also pursued a policy of mediation between competing Arab factions, (i.e., vis-a-vis the PLO) and frequently they have issued calls for Arab unity. Both leaders have tried to expand their dual roles as international statesmen and global revolutionaries. This has led to conflict and cooperation in the NAM and the U.N. While Qaddafi searches for pan-Arabism and the glory of Islam (with himself as figurehead), Castro seeks influence to bring home personal fulfillment; economic resources; expansion of Soviet objectives; and, consequently, an increase in Cuba's value to the Kremlin.

In Latin America, Libya and Cuba want to maintain and to propagate revolutionary regimes, especially in Central America (Nicaragua and El Salvador) and the Caribbean. To this end Libya devoted $200 million in arms to Central American guerrilla groups; loaned $100 million to Nicaragua; and reached a multimillion dollar trade agreement with the Sandinistas. Cuba granted financial assistance, training, and safe-haven in addition to military material.[3] Both countries seek to diminish U.S. power and cultivate friends in a region that traditionally has been conceived as the U.S. sphere of influence. Moreover, Cuba would gain by ending its ideological isolation in the Americas. At the same time, Libya would reap the pro-Arab (and the anti-Israeli) support of the revolutionary governments coming to power.

Lastly, on the international arena, Libyan and Cuban anti-Americanism has been operationalized in backing an assortment of leftist groups. Data on this topic, however, are difficult to find and verify. Disinformation and propaganda have tainted the available information. Yet, the Libyan-Cuban connection is an important one. It was working in the international forefront that Cuba and Libya first joined efforts, both directly and indirectly: directly, in the 1974 formation of the Revolutionary Coordinating Junta which has operated from the Cuban Embassy in Paris, partly on a Libyan budget, to assist Latin American revolutionary movements, indirectly, through support of the PLO.

HISTORY OF DIPLOMATIC RELATIONS

Cuba was one of the first countries to recognize the September Revolution that brought Qaddafi to power. Cuban recognition of the new military regime trailed the official Soviet message to the Revolutionary Council by several hours. On September 6, 1969 the island's Foreign Ministry publicly announced that Cuba had extended recognition to the Revolutionary Council in a pronouncement that had been sent to the Libyan leaders. The Ministry's communique added that the establishment of a republic in the North African state was an event of extraordinary historical significance.[4]

But the seeming initial fervor with which the new government had been received failed to produce any direct ambassadorial exchanges between Cuba and Libya. Between 1969 and 1973, the two countries did not maintain formal diplomatic relations. Commerical transactions, if occuring at all, were of marginal importance. Interestingly enough, Cuban sugar may have been reaching Libyan tables through a trade agreement with the Soviet Union. In early 1970, Libya signed a contract with the U.S.S.R. to purchase 25,000 tons of sugar at a cost of 2.25 million dollars.[5]

The fact that relations were not formalized during the first years of Qaddafi's rule is surprising considering Castro's overtures toward the Libyan leader. From 1969 to 1973 Havana applauded several of the major steps taken by Tripoli: the expulsion of U.S. air and naval bases from its territories, the decision "to arm the people" against U.S. aggression, and the nationalization of the petroleum industry.[6] Apparently, Qaddafi was not interested in Castro's support at this time. On the contrary, he might have felt threatened by Fidel's popularity and leadership in the NAM Qaddafi's Pan-Arabism and admiration for Nasser who was not receptive to Cuban involvement in the region might also help explain the distance between Tripoli and Havana.

During 1973, Libyan-Cuban relations took a turn for the worse. The possibility of establishing diplomatic representation between Tripoli and Havana seemed further away after the Non-Aligned countries gathered in Algiers in September of that year. It was during that conference that Castro and Qaddafi met face to face for the first time. Their encounter ended in an open confrontation that threatened to divide the Non-Aligned Movement.

At Algiers, Qaddafi claimed that the conference was not non-aligned "because regrettably the major international camps have managed to defeat the group of non-alignment."[7] This, and other of his comments, constituted an attack against Cuba's participation and Fidel's stature in the movement. Qaddafi contended that Cuba was in fact an ally of the Soviets, thus infiltrating the conference and undermining the main tenet of the movement. In reply to the Libyan leader, Castro labeled those who opposed the socialist countries' involvement in the Non-Aligned Movement counterrevolutionaries. The Cuban leader argued that the Soviet Union and the socialist bloc were the natural allies of the Third World. Only they could help the underdeveloped countries break the chains of capitalism and imperialism. Feeling the indirect attack, Colonel Qaddafi walked out in the middle of Castro's speech. At a press conference later that day (September 7, 1973), Qaddafi added that:

> We have no objection to the Cuban system, but we object to its presence among the non-aligned group because this presence is similar to the presence of any other Communist country such as Czechoslovakia or Hungary...The difference between Castro and me is that he is a Communist and I am a socialist. The object of the Cuban Revolution is Cuba's freedom. If freedom is to throw oneself in the lap of another state then this is alignment.[8]

Needless to say, the personal competition between Castro and Qaddafi for leadership of the NAM did not do much to foster the relations between the two countries.

The ensuing period between 1973 and 1977 was one of minimal diplomatic contacts. Neither state made any move to patch up the frayed situation after Algiers. The damage,

therefore, seemed to have lingered throughout these four years.
Given the strong personalities of both leaders, forgiving and
forgetting would have been construed as signs of weakness (be it
personal, political, or ideological). However, in 1976 Qaddafi
made a positive reference to Cuba and compared the "beseiged"
island to Libya. In a speech in which he lashed out at the forces
of imperialism (meaning in this case the U.S. and Egypt), the
Libyan leader praised the way Cuba "under Fidel survived under
the very nose of the United States" in spite of the CIA plots and
the U.S.-backed military interventions. He added that Fidel had
become an international figure, heading the struggle against the
reactionary powers of the world. Cuban assistance to the
Angolan fighters was offered as an example of the island's
support of progressive forces.[9]

The following year, 1977, marked a watershed in Cuban-
Libyan relations. Thanks to an invitation from the Libyan
government, Fidel spent ten days in March visiting the country
during his African tour. According to Yoram Shapira the
arrangements for the trip were made hastily, reflecting the
urgency of the visit for Colonel Qaddafi, who was finding
himself isolated in the Arab world.[10] The Cuban visit was to
coincide with a meeting in Cairo which Qaddafi was boycotting
and with the inauguration of the people's congress, an
institution similar to Cuba's *poder popular* (popular power).
Castro's visit would serve to legitimize Qaddafi's revolutionary
credentials in the Third World and would put Tripoli back in
the limelight.

During the ten days, Castro and the Cuban delegation
(which included such high-ranking members of the Central
Committee as Carlos Rafael Rodriguez) traveled throughout
Libya, visiting farms, factories, oil wells, and schools; conducting
closed-door meetings with the Qaddafi and the Prime Minister,
and even riding horseback with Qaddafi. The Cubans caught
the interest of the press and of the people. Popular rallies met
Fidel with shouts and banners throughout his tours. No other
world leader in the modern era has received such a warm (if
officially prepared) welcome; and no other head of state as far
as is known, has ever remained in Libya that length of time.
For countries such as Libya, where personalism and nationalism,
are deeply rooted and intertwined with revolution, Fidel was an
idol and a role model. Libya's first ambassador to Cuba
expressed great admiration for Fidel. In an interview with
Bohemia he stated that:

> To meet Fidel in flesh and blood, who we previously
> knew from third parties or from books, newspapers and
> magazines, was one of the major satisfactions of my life. I
> was able to assess him up close during his visit [to Libya

in 1977], in all his extraordinary capacity as a leader.
There are no words to express the impression that the
Commander in Chief left in all our people...[11]

Apparently Fidel's visit to Libya had one main purpose:
to strengthen ties between the two countries, which would, in
turn, fortify the front against global imperialism. For Qaddafi,
Fidel's visit validated his credentials as a global revolutionary
and inducted Libya into the fraternity of internationalist states.
Qaddafi needed Castro's approval at this time for he had
repeatedly failed in his regional and international aspirations.
Partnership with the Cubans would open doors for Libyan
foreign policy throughout the Third World and the entire globe.
From the moment of Fidel's arrival to Tripoli in 1977, the
two leaders showered each other with compliments and eulogies.
No trace of the Algerian animosity was publicly displayed. At
departure time, Fidel Castro claimed that: "We have come to
Libya as friends and we leave as brothers."[12] In return, Qaddafi
conferred the Order of Courage on Castro. Libya has also
awarded medals to several Cuban generals--Ulises Rosales del
Toro and Ramon Espinosa Martin--for their heroic efforts in
Africa.
The fraternal rhetoric was translated into practice via
two cooperation agreements signed. The first dealt with trade,
technology and economic matters; the second with scientific and
cultural exchanges. Reportedly, the two leaders agreed to trade
a Cuban military training mission in Libya for a quarter billion
dollar loan to be repaid in 1.9 million tons of sugar at the
current world prices. The loan was destined to finance Cuban
industrial development.[13] In addition, Castro and Qaddafi issued
a joint communique condemning Zionist Israel, reinforcing
Arab ties with the Third World (both leaders appointed
themselves spokesmen for a respective group of countries),
supporting socialism, non-alignment, NIEO, detente and several
revolutionary struggles. Before leaving Libyan soil, Castro
extended Qaddafi an invitation to visit his island, an offer that
Qaddafi accepted without setting a date.
Although the personal rapprochement occurred a year
after the countries had decided to establish official diplomatic
ties, Havana and Tripoli first exchanged ambassadors in 1977,
after Castro's trip. Cuba became the ninth Latin American
country to open relations with the Libyan *jamahiriya* (after
Argentina, Brazil, Chile, Costa Rica, Jamaica, Mexico, Panama,
and Venezuela). A new era of close cooperation thus began. In
1987 Cuba and Nicaragua rank at the top of Libya's Latin
American friends. Yet, Libyan-Nicaraguan relations are not
those of equal states (the Sandinistas' principal interest are
Qaddafi's petro-dollars and Soviet armory), while Cuban-Libyan

dealings resemble more closely those between partners where the need is mutual and the power is comparable and complementary.

What factors explain the developments of 1977? Qaddafi's turnabout from 1973 is striking. Even as late as 1976, in the Non-Aligned Conference at Colombo, the Libyan Colonel cautioned members of the movement against Trojan horses in their midst (a reference to Egypt, but possibly meaning Cuba as well).[14] In any case the rapprochement was both action and reaction to various situations prevalent in the Middle East and international context at that time, situations which limited or crushed Libyan foreign policy goals. 1977 presented a new set of circumstances for the North African country.

First, the OPEC-sponsored 1973 oil price hike flooded Libya with petro-dollars. Thanks to availability of hard currency and an abundance of reserves, Qaddafi could implement his foreign ambitions. Thus, he became the international revolutionary *nouveau riche*. Second, Egypt, the once powerful member of the long-dreamed-of Libyan-Arab union, had suddenly turned violently against both Qaddafi and the Soviet Union, redirecting its foreign policy toward the United States following the October War (1973). At the same time, U.S.-Libyan relations slowly deteriorated and were headed for a collision course. Finally, once Cuba's diplomatic relations with Israel had been cut in 1973, in his confrontation against the U.S. Castro could support Qaddafi.

Throughout this period, Libyan contact with the Soviet Union gradually became more frequent. The U.S.S.R. became Libya's major arm supplier. Cooperation in other areas (nuclear facilities, usage of ports, commerce) also increased. Possibly this paved the way for future Cuban-Libyan ties. Increase in Soviet weaponry brought with it a certain dependence that Qaddafi has always regarded cautiously. Cuban military technicians and advisers would prove to be a semi-panacea for the dangers of sole-reliance. Furthermore, in Castro, Qaddafi could find a bridge to reach Latin America, an area of expressed interest to the Libyan leader. Since 1973, Libya had openly announced the vital pressure that Latin America could exert to combat Zionism if it were courted by Arab nations:

> The Libyan Arab Republic has begun to attach great importance to the Latin American countries in view of the fact that they can play an important role in combating imperialism and Zionism. The director of Europe and the Two Americas' desk [of the Foreign Ministry] has clarified the Libya initiatives in creating strong links of cooperation and solidarity with the peoples of Latin America.[15]

Castro's international reputation had gained prominence with his Angolan and Ethiopian crusades, and his commanding performance as a leader of the Third World community. Qaddafi himself warmed up to Castro after the campaign in Angola and Ethiopia. The Libyan leader supported the deployment of Cuban troops in Africa and became increasingly interested in the possibility of using Cuban forces for his own foreign initiatives (i.e., against Egypt and or Chad). Associating with Fidel, a symbol of revolutionary success would be useful to Qaddafi, who has had a rather difficult time accomplishing his regional and global policy objectives.

For Cuba, a working relationship with Libya also conveyed certain political and economic advantages. Qaddafi's approval of Castro and the Cuban Revolution, could open the door to petro-dollars (much needed to reinvigorate the island's weak economy). Concurrently, Cuba's position vis-a-vis the Soviet Union would be strengthened if Fidel befriended Qaddafi. Since the Libyan Colonel has never fully accepted Marxism or an alliance with the U.S.S.R., Castro could eventually play the role of intermediary or power broker if any misunderstanding were to arise. Libya would provide Cuba with another place in which to expand its influence in the Middle East. And last, but not least, Castro would enhance his personal prestige and Cuba would magnify its image as the revolutionary powerhouse of the underdeveloped world.

The Cuban-Libyan conjunction furthers other mutual ideological and pragmatic interests. As mentioned, the two countries share several fundamental policy concerns and have close friends in common. Foremost, the blatant anti-Americanism of both countries is well served by this international collaboration. ("The front against imperialism," as Castro refers to it.) In addition, Qaddafi's and Castro's ideologies converge in other points, nationalism; concentration of power; militarization of society; controlled mass participation; and social change through revolution. Ideological affinity has been translated into catch all phrases such as anti-imperialism, anti-Zionism, anti-racism, and anti-colonialism. Secondly, the Caribbean island and the North African country have been deeply involved with many of the same countries and international groups for the past years: Syria, South Yemen, Ethiopia, Soviet Union, Iraq, Nicaragua, the PLO and others. Therefore, joining forces facilitated cooperation in third party states.

Since 1977 Castro has met with Qaddafi at least thrice: once in 1978 in Tripoli, as he returned home from an attempt to mediate the Eretrea-Ethiopia-Somalia imbroglio; later in 1981, at Brezhnev's funeral in Moscow; and in 1986, during the NAM ministerial meeting at Harare. (Neither Qaddafi or Jallud have visited Cuba). The topics covered during these meetings have included East and Central America, Israel and Zionism, and the U.S. policies. The purpose of the encounters has been to coordinate their positions and to plan joint actions. In Harare, Libya sought Cuba's endorsement for its proposal to include a condemnation of U.S. state terrorism into the draft political declaration of the N.A.M.

NATURE AND SCOPE
OF BILATERAL RELATIONS

Besides establishing embassies in the respective capitals, Cuban-Libyan cooperation has taken many forms. In general, the pattern conforms to traditional form of Cuban diplomacy with close friends: supplying paid technical and semi-technical personnel in various fields (from construction workers and doctors to military specialists); scholarships for study in Cuba; coordination of activities in international organizations; rhetorical support; and, ties with "progressive" regimes and movements around the globe. Political, military, and commercial dealings characterize the nature of their bilateral relations. The Libyan Arab-Cuban Economic and Social Cooperation Commission was organized to foster trade and cultural and scientific exchanges.

Commerical and financial cooperation has taken many forms, ranging from construction, agricultural, and industry to health and education. According to a Radio Havana broadcast of September 15, 1982, over 3,000 Cubans were employed in the construction, agricultural, and industrial sectors of the Libyan economy. Cuban workers are sent abroad in contracts arranged by the overseas sections of the Cuban ministries, including the Union of Caribbean Construction Enterprises (UNECA). Cubans have built 5 schools, a post office, a telephone exchange, and a 1,500 kilometer highway. Another contract stipulates the construction of 1,042 housing units. These sorts of transactions alleviate Cuban employment pressure while concurrently funneling much-needed foreign exchange into the island's bank. (Libya is one of the Arab countries which pays for Cuban development assistance.) For Libya, acquisition of skilled personnel fits into the state's development plans.[16]

Cuba has also been active in the fields of health and education. In 1978 Cuba agreed to send 650 medical personnel to Libya, of whom at least 245 were confirmed as having arrived.[17] In the educational field, Cuba has provided different sorts of technical (both civilian and military) and politico-ideological training. Radio Havana announced in 1982 that a number of

Libyan youth delegations would visit the island in 1983 to be trained in different areas of production.

Trade between both countries continues to be rather small; neither Cuba nor Libya figure as a main trading partner of the other. In June 1978 Libya promised to import sugar from Cuba.[18] No deals regarding oil trade have been reported.

Military cooperation has been an important aspect of Cuban Libyan relations. Since 1977 Cuban advisers and technicians have trained sections of the Libyan armed forces and serviced Soviet military equipment. Although numbers fluctuate, depending upon the source, it is likely that up to 1,000 Cuban "soldiers" or "technicians" have been in Libyan territory at the same time.[19] On November 9, 1978, Western observers claimed that "1,000 Cuban soldiers and hundreds of Soviet officers ... participated in Libyan ground and air maneuvers near Trobuk."[20] Unofficial reports (usually from Cairo) have denounced the presence of Cuban troops in Libya. (No evidence to substantiate this claim has been found to the present.) Others hint to the possibility that Cuba was intending to transport troops from Angola into Libya. Again, no hard facts verify this allegation. At one point Cairo reported 7,000 Cuban troops in Libya deployed along the Tunisian border.[21]

Cuban personnel have been involved in Libya's military establishment not only in servicing, advising, and training capacities, but also in intelligence and security work. Some reports indicate that Cuban advisers (teaming up with East Europeans) have helped in reorganization of the Libyan intelligence services and in the creation of an anti-putsch force.[22] Additional sources suggest that Cubans trained Colonel Qaddafi's personal bodyguards.[23]

One can conclude that Cubans have reached sensitive areas of the Libyan state bureaucracy. There have been inferences that due to the lack of confidence that Qaddafi has in the reliability of his army, Cubans could be placed in key positions if an emergency were to occur. Qaddafi has seen the need for Cuban military and intelligence expertise, particularly since he deems it wise to diversify his reliance on the Soviet military complex. Cuba, therefore, has become a useful political alternative which, while furnishing manifold benefits, reduces grave risks. An ever-deepening relationship with the Communist bloc would more than likely continue to alienate Qaddafi from many of his Arab brothers.

For Cuba, the export of services (and labor) is an inducement to cultivate relations with nations such as Libya which can afford to pay for Cuban international collaboration. The benefits to the island are multiple. First, the national bank receives much needed foreign exchange from such transactions. Second, sending workers abroad relieves domestic employment pressure. Third, and a speculative proposition, internationalist workers brigades may serve as channels to diffuse political tension before it builds up domestically (an export of national energy, if you will). Finally, socio-economic projects abroad build goodwill for Cuba among Third World countries and facilitate the reach and the success of the regime's foreign policy.

However, "internationalist duty" may eventually have negative repercussions for the political system. The diplacement of productive labor from their work place may lead to dislocations, lower productivity and economic costs. This, in turn, as others have suggested, may cause tension between the ideologists and the technocrats. At the level of support for the regime, the policy of internationalist duty has certain costs attached. The harsh living conditions of the brigadistas working in the Middle East and throughout the Third World may undermine their commitment to or their acceptance of the Revolution. A construction brigadista in Libya underscores the personal difficulties the Cubans encountered there:

> It is more than difficult here, but we always stand firm. All of us in Libya long for Cuba, we are surrounded by desert, we do not have where to go for entertainment at night, we do not understand the language and the customs are different from ours, but we do our job. When we arrived it was terrible.[24]

These words may veil latent opposition to, unhappiness with and alienation from the government's policies.

On regional and international issues, Libya and Cuba have a similar perspective. As a result, since 1977 they have supported each other on such questions as Israel's right to exist; Zionism as racism; tercermundismo (pro-Third World politics); Palestinian right to self-determination; South Africa; El Salvador; and Nicaragua. In areas closer to home, such as U.S. action against Cuba or Libya, both countries have expressed sympathy with the "victim" of U.S. imperialism. In 1981 in response to Reagan's policy toward Cuba, Qaddafi cabled his support to Fidel Castro and condemned U.S. propaganda against the island. One should remember that previously, in 1977, Qaddafi had pledged to defend Cuba in case of aggression.

Libya and Cuba spoke out against the U.S. invasion of Grenada. This common position was not without a slight hitch, for Libya deplored the Soviets' unwillingness to defend the tiny island-state. The situation is reminiscent of another one on which Castro and Qaddafi parted ways: Afghanistan. While Castro endorsed the Soviet intervention, the Libyan leader denounced it. This indicates that not all is smooth sailing between the two revolutionary colleagues. However, after the U.S. bombed Libya in 1986, the Cubans expressed solidarity with the Libyan people and Qaddafi sent an envoy to the island and other Latin American countries seeking support and asking for repudiation of U.S. actions.

LINKAGES

Cuba and Libya are joined to other states by ideological and strategic interests worldwide. Before inauguration of diplomatic offices, these two countries were dealing with one another indirectly through their support of third party countries. After 1977, the network was reinforced. The links are concentrated in two major regions of the world: Latin America (especially Central America) and the Middle East. Recent setbacks for Cuban policy in Grenada, Suriname, and Guyana have likely weakened these links, although an international connection remains in place.[25] The connecting links have been with the PLO, Syria, the PDRY, Ethiopia, Suriname (up to 1983), and the U.S.S.R. Ties and assitance to Nicaragua and the guerrillas in El Salvador have also brought Libya and Cuba together.[26]

Ironically, difference of opinions regarding course of action in third party states, specifically in El Salvador, might pull Qaddafi and Castro apart. According to *Foreign Report* the two leaders had a falling out in 1983 "over the strategy which the Salvadoran guerrilla forces ought to pursue."[27] *Foreign Report* adds that:

> While Castro has recently been urging the left-wing insurgents to seek negotiations rather than a purely military solution, Qaddafi believes they should aim solely at victory in a prolonged war. The disagreement is so sharp that when Qaddafi sent arms to the Salvadoran guerrillas via Nicaragua he dispatched them through Brazil and not Cuba, because he feared that Castro might hold on to them. The arms were blocked in Brazil. Castro may have tipped off the Brazilians about them.[28]

According to some sources, Libya and Cuba have supported a motley group of international terrorist organizations, varying from Tupamaros to the Japanese Red Army. Working hand in hand, in 1974 the two nations invited several Latin American Marxist guerrilla groups to join the Revolutionary Coordinating Junta, a committee housed at the Cuban Embassy in Paris designed to support terrorist and guerrilla activities. The Junta was partially financed by Libya.[29]

In addition, Libya and Cuba cooperated in building the airport at Pointe Salines in Grenada prior to the U.S. invasion. Maurice Bishop visited Libya in 1982 and became a friend of Qaddafi, who was willing to help foot the bill for the airport under construction. Castro supplied Cuban workers.

Although Cuban foreign activism has been restrained since the early 1980s, Havana (aided by Tripoli) may be supporting revolutionary groups in the Caribbean. In the East Caribbean, there is circumstantial evidence that links Castro and Qaddafi to a guerrilla group (the Revolutionary Army of the Caribbean or ARC) in Guadeloupe, Martinique, and French Guyana. The Movement's purpose is to end French colonialism in the area. Reportedly Libya and Cuba supply cash and weapons.[30]

PROSPECTS FOR CUBAN-LIBYAN RELATIONS AND IMPLICATIONS FOR THE U.S., LATIN AMERICA, AND THE MIDDLE EAST

The future for Cuban-Libyan relations, given no traumatic changes in the domestic situation of both states, is promising: a continuation of the path followed since 1977. This would entail cooperation in a variety of fields, marred by periodic conflicts between Qaddafi and Castro over what strategy to adopt in specific revolutionary situations. Several events have acted, and will continue to act, as constraints to the blossoming of collaboration. First, a downturn in oil prices has left Libya in an uncomfortable reserve position. Slush-funds to finance activities abroad will probably suffer cutbacks. Second, Cuba's reversal in Grenada and the apparent moderation of Suriname and other friendly states may weaken the Cuban-Libyan connection, as they have less friends in common, thus fewer places in which to cooperate. The continuing impasse in El Salvador, as well as Havana's and Tripoli's divergent positions regarding the resolution of the conflict, may also reduce cooperation between both countries.

Finally, Cuba's policy of neutrality, reconciliation, and mediation in the Middle East would seem to require a certain distance from Qaddafi's Libya, if the island's non-partisanship within inter-Arab disputes is to be sustained. Qaddafi, a conflictive leader in regional politics and a staunch ally of Iran, does not enjoy popularity in many Arab quarters. Fidel himself does not trust the Libyan leader, as evidenced by his refusal to send Cuban troops to Libya in 1977.[31] While Havana will maintain and develop its relations with Tripoli, it will avoid embracing Qaddafi's plans as its own. Therefore, cooperation will be selective, which shows moderation and pragmatism on the part of Cuban foreign policy. Above all, prospects for further association and joint ventures will be determined by the costs and benefits for both parties, and, in the Cuban case, the positive ripple effect of such for the Soviet Union as well. Given the pattern of clashes between Qaddafi and Castro the Cuban-Libya relationship will always be vulnerable to unexpected predicaments.

Cuban policy in Libya is evidence of the complexity of Cuban-Soviet interaction in the Third World. Havana's policy toward Tripoli is not autonomous or subordinated to Moscow, but is a combination of both, and reflects a convergence of interests between Cuba and the Soviet Union. Neither the Soviets or the Cubans could have pursued a far reaching policy acting alone as they have been able to do working together. Qaddafi's nationalistic and personalistic tendencies have posed obstacles to the involvement of foreign powers in Libya. He has diversified his friends and patrons so as not to rely too heavily on one. For instance, while the Soviets supply Qaddafi's armory, the Cubans service it and train Libyans on how to use Soviet weaponry. The division of labor brings benefits to all parties concerned: to the Libyans, reduction in dependence on the U.S.S.R.; to the Soviets, expansion influence, indirectly through the Cubans; and to the Cubans, room for a global foreign policy which not only fulfills Castro's ideological objectives but brings tangible rewards to the island as of result of trade, export of services, and the island's increased value to the Kremlin.

NOTES

1. For a general discussion of Libyan domestic and foreign policies see John K. Cooley, *Libyan Sandstorm: The Complete Account of Qaddafi's Revolution* (New York: Holt, Rinehart and Winston, 1982).

2. On Libya, see Jacques Roumani, "From Republic to Jamahiriya: Libya's Search for Political Community," *The Middle East Journal*, 37 (Spring 1983).

3. United States Department of State, "The Sandinistas and Middle Eastern Radicals, (mimeo) August 1985, pp. 5,7. See also "Nicaragua expects aid from Libya and Cuba," *The Christian Science Monitor*, 27 April 1981, p. 2.

4. F.B.I.S., *Africa and the Middle East*, September 5, 1969.

5. F.B.I.S., *Africa and the Middle East*, April 2, 1970.

6. See *Bohemia*, 65 (25) 22 June 1973, p. 80.

7. Ibid., Supplement, September 25, 1973.

8. Ibid.

9. F.B.I.S., *Africa and the Middle East*, 4 April, 1976.

10. Yoham Shapira, "Cuba and the Arab-Israeli Conflict" in Cole Blasier, ed., *Cuba in the World* (Pittsburgh: University of Pittsburgh Press, 1979) p. 161.

11. *Bohemia*, 69 (35): 68-69, 2 September 1977, p. 69.

12. Legum and Shaked, eds., Vol. III, p. 703.

13. William Durch, "The Cuban Military in Africa and the Middle East: From Algeria to Angola," *Studies in Comparative Communism*, (Spring-Summer 1978): 72.

14. F.B.I.S., *Africa and the Middle East*, April 4, 1976.

15. Ibid., July 2, 1973.

16. *Juventud Rebelde*, 3 August, 1983, p. 4; *Cuba Internacional*, July 1983, and Legun, Colin, and Haim Shaked, eds., *The Middle East Contemporary Survey*, Vol. II, (1977-78), New York: Holmes and Meir, 1978, p. 645.

17. Legum and Shaked, eds., Vol. III.

18. Ibid., Vol. II, p. 645.

19. Legum and Shaked, eds., Vol. III, p. 703.

20. U.S. Government, *Libya: A Country Study* (Washington: U.S. Printing Office, 1979) p. 265.

21. Ibid.

22. Ibid.

23. Wright, p. 202.

24. *Bohemia*, Vol. 75, No. 36, 9 September 1983, pp. 79-80, 82.

25. See McColm.

26. Bruce R. McColm, "Central America and the Caribbean: The Larger Scenario," *Strategic Review*, Vol. (Summer 1983):28-42.

27. *Foreign Report*, 11 August 1983, p.8.

28. Ibid.

29. See Mark Siljander, "The Palestine Liberation Organization in Central America," (mimeo) October 1983.

30. *The Miami Herald*, March 11, 1985, p. F2.

31. Interview with Juan Benemelis, Miami, November 8, 1985. Benemelis's assertion is confirmed in *Libya: A Country Study*, p. 265.

5

Cuban Foreign Policy
in the Middle East: Conclusions

In the Middle East, Cuba has pursued a policy which is extensive and influential. The island's reach in the region is considerable, having close contact with many of the regimes in power. For a small, underdeveloped country far removed from North Africa and the Arabian peninsula, the feat is nothing short of startling. In the Mid-East, Havana is playing a game of high diplomacy usually reserved for regional actors or great powers. But the extent of Cuban-Arab ties is not the only surprising dimension of the island's involvement in the region. The qualitative aspects of Cuba's foreign policy are as remarkable.

Although longstanding tenets of Castro's ideology are reaffirmed in the regime's activities in the Middle East, Cuba's conduct there has been uncharacteristic. The reason for the uniqueness of Cuban activites in the Middle East is that the means and ends of foreign policy have been adapted to the politics of the area. By adapting to the conditions prevalent in the Arab world and those surrounding the Arab-Israeli conflict, Cuba has attempted to reduce the high risks associated with involvement in an explosive region of the world. In the Middle East, Fidel Castro has turned to pragmatism as a way of implementing foreign policy while remaining faithful to the principles of Castroism, a masterful combination.

One of the striking features of Castro's approach to the Arab-Israeli conflict and to the Middle East in general has been its duality. On the one hand, Havana has been increasingly vocal in its opposition to Israel (although diplomatic relations lasted until 1973) and has taken a firm stand against what she perceives as reactionary (pro-U.S.) states in the area (i.e., Saudi Arabia, Egypt under Sadat, and Oman among others). On the other hand, the island has opted to remain neutral in conflicts involving revolutionary groups, countries, and-or factions. The definition of what constitutes revolutionary has been broad and flexible, covering such diverse (and at times staunch anti-Marxists) as Algeria, Iran, Iraq, Syria, Libya, the PDRY (including several elite factions competing for power), and the major PLO groups. Cuba's policy has been one of straddling the fence while calling for unity among Arab brothers. This approach has been a wise one given the factional nature of Arab politics. Rather than choosing sides among the contending progressive (i.e., anti-status quo) forces, Castro has decided to play the role of mediator, a friend of all who espouse anti-Americanism, anti-imperialism, and radical change.

The island's dual policy, (inter-Arab mediation, neutrality, and conciliation combined with strident anti-Israeli and anti-conservative Arab posture) has been the result of ideological and pragmatic considerations: (1) anti-Americanism and anti-imperialism; (2) concern for Soviet objectives and interests; and, (3) maximization of Cuban interests. For Cuba, the role of middleman offers considerable advantages. First, it allows Cuba to keep old friends. Second, it lays the groundwork for the expansion of influence in the region. Third, it reduces the risks and costs of having to side with one camp or the other, and choosing the wrong, or losing, side. No-win situations such as the one Cuba experienced in the Somalia-Ethiopia dispute are avoided. For the Soviets, Cuban mediation opens opportunities for influence as well. The Soviets, by remaining in the background and not becoming directly involved in regional disputes, appear less threatening to the Arabs and, at the same time, keep doors open to conservative Arab nations and even to Israel.

Mediation and neutrality are the best course for a successful Cuban policy in the region. Straddling fences, however, has not been characteristic of revolutionary foreign policy except in the Middle East. The emphasis on diplomacy, negotiation, and conflict resolution as *modus operandi* is indicative of a shift in Cuba's international behavior from military internationalism to high level diplomacy and from a foreign policy dominated by ideology to one molded by pragmatism.

Mediation requires flexibility. Havana has attempted to appear ideologically flexible so as to become an acceptable mediator to diverse groups. The tactic has paid off; Cuba has mediated between Iran and Iraq; PLO factions; PDRY power contenders; the PLO and Syria; Aden and Moscow; and, between Arab groups in the Non-Aligned Movement (NAM). However, pragmatism and flexibility have not overtaken the ideological underpinnings of Cuban foreign policy and the principles of Castroism. While the tactics are pragmatic, the strategy is ideological. Cuba's actions in the region, in spite of their unique characteristic, reflect a commitment to the pillars of Castroism as defined by Andres Suarez.

While Castroism is the driving force behind Cuba's international relations, it is, at the same time, tempered by a practical awareness of Cuba's limitations, and by the need to staisfy Soviet interests. In the lider maximo's view of the world, economic considerations are secondary but still are necessary to maintain power at home, as well as to project it abroad. Therefore any economic gain acquired in the process of, or as the result of, Cuban initiatives overseas are not only welcome, but sought after, for they facilitate Cuba's independence from, and lessen its dependence upon, the Soviet Union.

The Cuban leadership is pragmatic enough to accept the preeminence of the Soviet Union in certain areas of the world, such as the Middle East, where Havana acknowledges Moscow's right to a commanding role. Fortunately for both parties, ideology and practicality converge sufficiently to make their joint, albeit unequal, ventures advantageous to both sides.

While Castro sets the ideological parameters, various organs of the state bureaucracy are granted considerable autonomy in the conduct of their affairs with Middle Eastern counterparts. This is true of the Ministry of Construction Abroad, for example, as well as for the FAR, among other state agencies and PCC departments. Cuban foreign policy functions as a two-tier phenomenon. The first level of ideology and policy guidelines is determined solely by Fidel Castro with the advise, consent, participation and knowledge of a small inner group of longtime friends. The second level, concerned with the application and implementation of the first tier's decisions and principles, is left largely to the discretion of technocrats, civilians, soldiers, and other bureaucratic professionals, although Fidel can intervene in the process at any time and does so frequently. Theoretically the two levels reinforce and complement one another, although, in practice, they could contradict one another should ideological commitments run counter to more practical requirements. Grenada would be an instance of this sort of contradiction arising from conflicting orders from the top tier (Fidel) and the secondary tier (the Cubans in Grenada).

RISKS, OPTIONS, CONSTRAINTS

Cuba's entrance into Middle East politics has introduced new risks into its foreign policy in return for whatever benefits have been derived. More than other areas of Cuban involvement, the Middle East is a region where Cuba's policies and political objectives could easily be overtaken by events and the Cuban leaders could find themselves losing control of issues and intended outcomes. However, until 1987, Cuba has been successful in following limited but incremental contacts with the Middle East. Cuba's policy has laid the basis for further involvement, if it so desires, but external and internal constraints reduce this possibility.

One category of risk stems from the domestic political frailty of many of the regimes they support. Political infighting within the top leadership is a common characteristic of many Arab countries, lending an element of uncertainty to inter-state relations. Factionalism jeopardizes the unity of the PLO, the PDRY, and even possibly Libya. Fragmentation has led to civil war in Lebanon. The governments of Syria, Kuwait, and Iraq rest on narrow political bases, which make them particularly vulnerable to conflicts within the leadership as well as to popular pressures.

Not only do such regional dynamics pose hazards for Cuban objectives in the area but they also raise the cost of its involvement there as well. Antagonism between countries, such as between Iran and Iraq, and between North and South Yemen, create difficulties for outside actors who feel pressured into the unpalatable alternatives of either choosing sides or steering a middle course between the two. Guessing "wrong" can limit options or lead to diminished influence under the best of circumstances. Diplomacy must proceed cautiously, either to avoid the dilemma of a Catch-22 situation or the misfortune of ending up on the losing side of a dispute. This is exactly the course Cuba has followed.

Another category of risk stems from superpower involvement in the Middle East. Activities and interests of both the United States and the Soviet Union create risk factors for Cuba. First, any Cuban military enterprises in the area run the risk of encountering either U.S. or Israeli resistance. Second, while the Soviet relationship with the more radical Mid East states serves as the model and framework for Cuban relations with the same countries, it can also serve as a mixed blessing of a sort and hence as constraint. For instance, any Arab mistrust of the Soviets may well translate into comparable mistrust of the Cubans. To the extent that Arab leaders perceive Cuba to be a surrogate for the Soviets, they may well be apprehensive of its actions and suspicious of its motives.

The island's alliance with the U.S.S.R. carries with it other constraints as well, not least of which is that of their common ideology. Domestically, Arab states have repressed, even decimated, their communist parties. Soviet intervention on behalf of Marxist organizations and their leaders in certain cases only served to exacerbate the situation. This only

underlines the fact that, although mideast governments may
want arms, supplies and other kinds of support from the
Kremlin, they do not want any meddling in their internal affairs
or domestic politics. The twin factors of nationalism and Islam
combine to act as a formidable deterrrent to any major
expansion of Soviet-Cuban influence.

Both the Cubans and the Soviets have tried to encourage
the Arabs to adopt a common stance against the United States
and its "imperialism." On the ideological level, the two allies
divide the countries of the Middle East into two camps: (1)
progressive and (2) reactionary. Recently, the rhetoric directed
against the reactionary (i.e., conservative) states of Saudi Arabia,
Kuwait, Jordan, and North Yemen has been considerably toned
down in an effort to improve relations with them and with
other moderate nations. The effort to create a common Arab
front with which to oppose the United States has thus far failed,
due primarily to internal divisions among the Arabs themselves.

The Soviets have been unable to utilize the inter-Arab
crises to further their own ends, mostly because they present the
dilemma of no-win type situations. If Moscow starts out to help
one party in a local conflict, it finds itself in a position to injure
another. Out of desire to make a friend, the Kremlin *ipso facto*
makes an enemy. In an effort to resolve the predicament posed
by conflict, the Cubans have been enlisted to act as mediators:
to attempt to bring unity to sparring, if not warring, groups. It
is unlikely, however, that Cuban efforts can suceed in resolving
differences long ingrained and emanating from religious, ethnic,
ideological and personal roots.

The post-Nasser generation of Arab leaders has never
manifested the admiration for the U.S.S.R. displayed by their
predecessors. First, Marxism, as a philosophy, has encountered
setbakcs in intellectual circles throughout the world. Second, a
basic tenet of the Soviet state, state monopoly of the means of
production, has failed to produce the economic miracles
originally predicted. Third, the Soviets have fallen behind in
the technology race in comparison with other countries. Fourth,
Soviet culture has never managed to generate the mass appeal
that western consumer culture has commanded. Fifth, the
Soviet invasion of Afghanistan brought home to the current
generation of Arabs the potential for Soviet aggressive
penetration of the region. The result is that countries who were
once staunch supporters of the Soviet Union now flirt with the
western bloc. Syria and Iraq, for instance, have both indicated
interest in some degree of rapprochement with the United
States and western Europe. Post-Nasser Egypt has expelled its
Soviet advisers, severed diplomatic relations with the U.S.S.R.,
and generally followed a pro-U.S. course in recent years Under

Hosni Mubarak Egyptian-Soviet relations have experienced a minor thaw.[1]

Finally, as Cuba's involvement in the Middle East expands, the Castro regime will have to confront another category of risks. Factionalism within the island's Arab friends may well provoke and exacerbate fragmentation within within the Cuban foreign policy establishment. It is not unusual that as relations between states develop, different individuals and bureaucracies forge links with diverse, and at times contending, groups in the other country. Alliances are formed and preferences are established. In the case that Havana, faced with civil strife abroad, receives conflicting signals from the various Cuban bureaucracies involved in that country, the decision on whom to support and what course to pursue will be a difficult one. Taking such a choice could cause intra-elite friction, for not all groups of the Cuban foreign policy apparatus will be accommodated. Such a scenario is all but unrealistic, as events in South Yemen have demonstrated.

CUBAN-SOVIET INTERACTION

The fact that Cuba's policy is intertwined with that of the Soviet Union means that: (a) it inherits some of the same problems and constraints that face the Soviets in the region; while, (b) it tries to function independently of them, sometimes assuming roles (i.e., that of peacemaker and or broker) which the Soviets cannot perform either at all, or with as much credibility; (c) it receives Soviet military and economic assistance necessary for "big power" foreign activities; and, (d) it is provided with the groundwork or opportunities to establish ties with countries friendly to the Soviets.

Up til now, Cuba's policy has embraced a principal Soviet goal, that of finding a role for the Kremlin in negotiating any peace settlement in the region. Thus Cuba's efforts to play the part of honest broker in resolving either hostilities or divisiveness in the Arab camp was motivated, in part, by the objective of finding an opening for Soviet input, either directly or by proxy, into a modus vivendi or in the ongoing negotiations for a peace settlement.

The Cubans are useful to the Soviets in a military sense as well. As Lutwak has pointed out, in those countries of the Arabian peninsula which possess small military establishments, the outcome of a conflict could be decided by the addition of only a couple of hundred Cuban advisers.[2] Such Cuban assistance tends to work in favor of Soviet interests, as was the case in Angola and Ethiopia. Transporting Cuban troops from Africa to the Middle East, by way of South Yemen, is but a short maneuver, and one which the Cubans undertook in reverse in 1977, when they transported troops from Aden to Ethiopia.

Soviet aid to Arab states has not automatically translated into extensive influence for Moscow.[3] The same logic applies to Cuba. Nationalism, xenophobia, the will to be in control, and apprehension of the Soviet bloc all combine to limit the ability of outside powers to influence decision-making. This, of course, is a matter of degree. Although Cuba may have influence in certain circles and with certain individuals, leaders of Arab states pursue their own interests. They may avail themselves of Cuban aid and align themselves with the Soviet Union when they have something to gain by doing so, but they always reserve the right to back off when it serves their purpose. Cuban military missions, nevertheless, may have forged bonds between the FAR and the Arab armies which give the Cuban and the Soviets leverage over them.

The Soviets have experienced their share of setbacks in the Middle East region. David Andelman describes Soviet failures as "a complex amalgam of military, political, and diplomatic errors and, in some cases, simply bad luck–choosing the wrong side, the inept players, failing to seize the tactical moment."[4] This assessment has serious implications for Cuba. Given their dismal record, the Soviets find it expedient to encourage Cuba's role as proxy. For Castro, however, orchestrating his policy with the Kremlin's increases his risks. Following the Soviet lead in the Middle East can place the Cubans in awkward, if not dangerous, situations.

Since the war in Lebanon (1982), the pro-Soviet alignment in the Middle East has shown signs of wavering. Syria has evinced some friendly dispositions toward the West but remains strongly attached to the Soviet camp just the same, mostly for lack of any other real alternative. It has a treaty of friendship with the Soviets, providing for defense and security assistance, which binds the two nations – and no other nations has indicated its willingness to satisfy Syria's military or economic needs. Iraq has manifested displeasure at the inability of the U.S. and the U.S.S.R. to put an end to the war in the Persian Gulf. Even Baghdad feels pressure from the Soviets as the latter insists upon hard currency payment for Soviet weaponry in a war which is costing almost $1 billion a month. To complicate matters further, Soviet leaders have refused to come out with a strong pro-Iraqi position, and it is known that Soviet arms have reached Khomeini's troops through Syria. Although about 2,000 Soviet and East European troops are stationed in Iraq, there are signs that Soviet influence there is on the wane. First, Saudi Arabia has supplied President Hussein with arms and credits, thus partially displacing the U.S.S.R. Second, Iraq has moderated its anti-American rhetoric considerably. Third,

Iraq was among those nations who went on record to condemn the Soviet invasion of Afghanistan. Finally, Iraq supported the Fez Peace Plan, to which the Soviets reacted ambiguously.[5]

Meanwhile, the crisis within PLO leadership and the antagonism between Arafat and (Syria's) Al'Assad may serve to distance the organization from Moscow, if a settlement is not found.[6] Faced with these prospects, especially if the drift continues, the Soviet Union may find itself increasingly forced to exert its influence indirectly, through Cuba. In 1986 and 1987, in fact, Cuba played an increasing role in bringing together the various PLO factions.

Havana's dependence upon Moscow does limit its options. Castro, however, in an effort to reduce risks and to save face with the Arabs, has pursued seemingly independent initiatives, such as those involving mediation and or pursuit of peace. These initiatives reflect the convergence of Cuban-U.S.S.R. interests at the same time they allow Cuba room for independent action. In this way Cuba-Soviet interaction in the Middle East is able to fuse the three elements of dependence, independence and convergence. The fusion maximizes benefits to both parties and reduces the risks to each, an especially useful fromula.

Finally, as other issues compete for priority on the Soviet agenda, Havana may find itself increasingly called upon to "mind the store" of Soviet interests in the Middle East. Rival issues may claim greater share of Soviet attention in the near term, relegating the Middle East to the area of secondary concern: post-succession political maneuverings and economic problems within the U.S.S.R.; glaznot; arms control negotiations with the U.S.; accommodation with China; control over Poland; the war in Afghanistan, to name but a few. Temporarily, and partially, Cuba may be pressed to fill the vacuum. In this case, again, the Soviets would set the parameters for Cuban activities.

DOMESTIC BENEFITS AND COSTS

Cuba has derived definite benefits from its Middle Eastern policy. The island's economy suffers from unemployment and underemployment, and thus finds in the Middle East a market for the export of human capital. By providing professional and blue-collar workers as trainers, advisers, or as skilled workers on various technical and economic development projects, Cuba is enabled to relieve its domestic labor pressure. If the recipient countries also happen to be rich oil-producers, the regime can also earn much-needed foreign exchange (e.g., Libya and Algeria). By developing relations with the Arab world, Castro may hope to be able to lessen his dependence upon the Soviet Union for trade, particularly as regards oil. There are also hopes that capital-exporting countries of the region can be encouraged to enter into joint ventures with Cuba.[7]

Exporting surplus labor also serves political purposes, diffusing popular pressure on the Cuban government. Sending workers abroad may create other sorts of domestic conflicts, such as popular opposition to the regime from individuals who would prefer not to carry out internationalist duty. By developing relations with the Arab world, Castro may hope to be able to lessen his dependence upon the Soviet Union for trade, particularly as regards oil. There are also hopes that capital-exporting countries of the region can be encouraged to enter into joint ventures with Cuba. Loans from Arab banks and the recent emphasis on increasing trade with the Middle East point to Cuba's growing interest on the economic side of relations with the region.

Aside from the opportunity for increasing economic gains from countries of the Middle East, Cuba stands to gain from the Soviet Union as well: furthering Soviet goals in the region can bring both material rewards as well as, or as a result of, increased leverage with Moscow. If one is to judge from Cuban experiences in Angola and Ethiopia, the U.S.S.R. compensates generously for assistance rendered by granting of new trade agreements and in supplying advanced military equipment. The economic agreements signed in 1983 are an example of this payoff effect.[8] The continuation of trade concessions, rescheduling of debt, and acceleration of weapons deliveries all testify to entrenched Soviet support for Cuba's revolutionary elite. It is not clear if the extent of subsidies, gifts, loans, and other special treatment will continue or shrink in the future. Soviet backing insures the survival of the regime which, after all, is the paramount objective of Cuba's foreign policy.

Given the nature of Cuban activities in the Mid East, costs have been kept to a minimum so far. The present emphasis on diplomacy and development assistance (paid or unpaid) reduces the risk of untenable, costly commitments, particularly of a military nature. The number of personnel involved in military missions has remained relatively stable in the recent past (1980-85), thus limiting both the role of the FAR as well as liabilities to the system. So long as military aid and deployment of troops does not become a cornerstone of Cuba's Mid-East policy, the potential for incurring more serious costs remains within limits.

The majority of Cuban overseas workers are also FAR reservists and, as such, constitute a small fighting force if needed. In the event that a local conflict should erupt, *a la* Grenada, they are expected to fight to the end. Thus military advisers and instructors, such as those now stationed in Algeria, Syria, South Yemen, Libya, and Iraq, could be expected to take part in any fighting that might arise. As things now stand, Cuban military forces serve primarily as a reinforcement to regimes in power in the event of a coup from within. The Cuban military presence in the Mid East does not have sufficient strength to present any threat to Israel, for example.[9]

In the event of any major military involvement, a rash of casualties and escalation of militarization would cause friction within the Cuban elite and the state and party organs. Additional commitments abroad would act to increase the economic and political costs to the regime, as has been the case with the African campaigns. Domestic costs associated with any large-scale military engagement are sufficiently high as to reduce the attraction--or probability--of any such undertaking. Therefore it seems likely that Cuba will continue to pursue a prudent, low-profile policy, one which emphasizes high diplomacy, mediation, socio-economic cooperation over military commitment, at least in the foreseeable future. This policy track will be accompanied by support for national liberation groups whenever possible, as the cases of Oman and Bahrain indicate.

CUBAN FOREIGN POLICY
IN THE MIDDLE EAST:
IMPLICATIONS AND PROSPECTS

To the Middle East, Cuba represents an agent of Soviet interests, on the one hand, and another external actor (with its own agenda) contributing to the internationalization of regional conflict, on the other. Cuba's activities there are fundamentally intended to oppose, or undermine, Israel and the interests of the United States. Cuba's closest allies are members of the Steadfastness and Confrontation Front, and Cuban policies are designed to strengthen those radical states. However, Cuba does not have the capability to effect any significant change in the correlation of military forces involved in the Israeli-Arab confrontation. What Cuba can do, and has been doing, is (1) to mediate inter-Arab conflicts and encourage reconciliation; and (2) to provide military and para-military services such as training Arabs in the use of Soviet weaponry and servicing Soviet equipment. While deployment of Cuban troops, even at the levels lower than that of Angola or Ethiopia, appears highly unlikely at present, this option can never be wholly ruled out.

On one level, the Cuban presence complicates the Arab-Israeli conflict by adding to the number of participants. The internationlization of the crisis might complicate its resolution.

On another level Cuba's efforts to unify Arab factions and countries through mediation can strenghten the Arab side and enhance prospects for confrontation against Israel. In either case, the prospect for peace in the region would be dim. However, Cuba's lobbying and mediation efforts on behalf of a U.N. sponsored peace conference may be a step toward negotiated Arab-Israeli settlement.

Cuba's incursion into the Middle East has had global, not only regional, repercusions. Cuba has served Arab countries as a bridge to Latin America. Havana has opened doors to Arab groups (such as the PLO) and states (such as Libya) who have been interested in establishing and expanding contacts with Central and South America. While Cuban presence in the Middle East contributes to the internationalization of the Arab-Israeli conflict, a similar internationalization of the Central American crisis has occurred, partly due to Cuba's middleman role.

Current political trends in Cuba suggest that past Middle East policies will continue. Havana will seek to increase its role in the region, especially through mediation of conflict and socio-economic projects. Since the mid-1980s the island has shown a renewed interest and commitment to the Middle East, as recent efforts to settle PLO disputes, increase trade with Arab countries, and reorganize the North Africa and Middle East section of the Ministry of Foreign Relations reveal. Cuba's actions during 1986 and 1987 signal the beginning of a diplomatic offensive in the area, which might or might not come to fruition. What is clear is that the Cubans are interested in securing their role as important backstage figures in the Middle Eastern drama. However, various factors militate against expansion of its role there: the foreign policy defeats abroad ("loss" of Grenada, and widespread disapproval of Cuban support for Soviet invasion of Afghanistan, among others) which have served to diminish influence and credibility; and, the uncertain future of continuing major overseas commitments (in Nicaragua, Ethiopia, and, painfully, Angola). The loss of Cuban prestige within the Non-Aligned Movement limits what it can hope to accomplish through that body. Past failures in shuttle diplomacy and mediation efforts might also act against Cuba's desire to deepen its involvement.

While there is room for a mediator in the region, practical conditions would seem to limit Cuba's prospects for other sorts of involvement in the Middle East. Cuba's closest friends (Syria, the PDRY) in the region are not the rich countries and or are waging costly wars (Iraq). Libya would appear to represent the only potential source of funds, yet its track record and recent economic setbacks are discouraging. Except for human capital and sugar, Cuba has little to offer to the countries of the Middle East; nor do the Arab states produce anything needed by the Cubans, with the single, and important, exception of oil. Cuba can, however, provide military assistance and training, although someone, either the Arabs or the Soviets, must cover the costs. Therefore, the future of Cuba's policy toward the area rests largely outside Castro's control. Either the Arab countries or the Soviet Union must request deeper Cuban involvement. Up to now, both the Soviet and the Arabs have accepted, and even encouraged, Cuba's mediating function.

Oil is, of necessity, one of Castro's prime concerns. The present Soviet supplier is apparently tired of subsidizing the island's energy needs and has begun to call for greater efficiency, if not austerity.[10] Moscow is making it clear that it does not intend to foot the bill forever; recently, the Soviets denied the Cuban's request for lower oil prices and higher subsidy for sugar. Soviet displeasure is not loss upon Castro, who still remembers the tight situation he faced in 1967 when the Soviet Union decided to delay its oil shipments to the island. Therefore, the possibility of diversifying Cuba's suppliers of oil is appealing. However, this is not easy. It is unlikely that individual members of OPEC are ready to supply Cuba with oil at below world market prices. Qaddafi could be induced to demonstrate his revolutionary solidarity by supplying Cuba with oil, especially if the Soviets raise the price of its oil exports to the island. But how will Cuba pay for oil shipments without loans from the Soviets? Iraq, on the other hand, is mired in a war that costs its regime millions of dollars and therefore is in no position to settle for anything less than top dollar for its commodity. Cuba will not find an oil deal in the Middle East comparable to the one it has enjoyed with the Soviet Union. Furthermore, Cuba's oil needs could best be satisfied by Mexico or Venezuela, close neighbors.

A further constraint upon Cuban activism has been the commitment of the United States, under the Reagan Administration, to halt the spread of "communism" wherever possible. The effect has been to nudge Castro toward more prudent, diplomatic, and, at times, low-profile initiatives. As Castro has tuned his global policy to outside factors, he has rediscovered his Caribbean and Latin neighbors and, he has increasingly settled for undertakings that are relatively risk-free yet sufficiently prestigious to satisfy his great-statesman yearnings as much as possible. One way to accomplish this has been to organize, and host, continental conferences (such as the two on the debt crisis) which attract the attention and provide the platform he requires. Meanwhile experience suggests it is both prudent, and cheaper, to rely less upon military instruments of foreign policy such as the FAR, and more upon diplomatic means, such as negotiation, mediation, and civilian trainers and advisers.

The complexities and the importance of Middle Eastern politics will continue to fascinate and attract Fidel Castro and Cuba. More than any other region, the Middle East provides the arena for the lider maximo to cap his international statesman career and fulfill his global aspirations. The Arab-Israeli conflict; superpower contention in the area; the strategic significance of the Arabian peninsula and its principal product, oil; as well as inter-Arab disputes are magnets which pull Castro and his regime to shores far away from the Caribbean. The opportunity to score an anti-American coup and reap international prestige for himself and his country becons Fidel to the Arab world. This zeal has been tempered by the recognition that flexibility and prudence are necessary, for the risks are high. The solutions to the regional problems are not easy, and Soviet guidelines must be followed. Therefore, Cuba will proceed between cautious and deeper involvement in the area, pursuing an agenda which no other Third World state has carried out and placing itself in a position to make a difference when the time comes. The Middle East might well be Fidel Castro's, and revolutionary Cuba's, last international frontier, pointing to old and new dimensions of Cuban foreign policy, signalling an end and a beginning.

NOTES

1. This discussion is based on Aryeh Y. Yodfat, *The Soviet Union and The Arabian Peninsula*, (London: Croom Helm 1983).

2. For a lengthy discussion see Edward Lutwak, "Cubans in Arabia? or the Meaning of Strategy," *Commentary* 68 (December 1979): 62-66.

3. Yodfat, p. 26.

4. Davis A. Andelman, "Andropov's Middle East," *The Washington Quarterly* 6 (Spring 1983): 111.

5. Ibid.

6. Ibid., pp. 112-113.

7. For a discussion of Cuba's joint venture law, see Jorge F. Perez-Lopez, "The 1982 Cuban Joint Venture Law: Context, Assessments and Prospects," (Miami: Institute of Interamerican Studies Monograph July 1985).

8. Edward Gonzalez defends this "pay-off" point of view. See his "Complexities of Cuban Foreign Policy." *Problems of Communism* (November-December 1977).

9. See Lutwak.

10. For a complete account of Cuba's energy problems and recent Soviet pressure for austerity see *The Latin American Report* during 1984-1985.

Appendix A

On the question of Cuban-Soviet interaction in foreign policy, Carmelo Mesa-Lago has offered a useful framework to analyze the regime's activities abroad. He has summarized the patterns that characterize Cuba's foreign initiatives as follows:

1) Cuba's foreign policy is highly dependent in relation to regionsicountriesiissues which are vital to the U.S.S.R. particularly when they affect Soviet national security.

2) Cuba's foreign policy is more independent in relation to regionsicountriesiissues which are less vital to Soviet national security, and interests.

3) Even in situations of independence, Cuba's space for action is often conditioned by Soviet support or influence and is clearly limited by any potential threat to Soviet national security.

4) In general, and with the limitations explained above, Cuban foreign policy tends to be more daring than Soviet foreign policy.

This framework may be used as a starting point to analyze Cuba's Middle East policy, providing a context to which Cuba's behavior may be related. Furthermore, the island's policy in the Middle East is a study case which reveals additional variables which must be included when analyzing Cuban-Soviet interaction.

The study of Cuba's policy in the Middle East indicates that future studies should consider additional variables to explain Cuban-Soviet interaction in the Third World. In addition to Mesa Lago's propositions, the determinant variables of autonomy, convergence, or subordination seem to be: (1) time (length of Cuban presence compared to length of Soviet presence); (2) *regime type*; (divided into two categories which are

129

not mutually exclusive between each other: personalistic versus collective leadership and aligned versus non-aligned countries); (3) factionalism (bureaucratic politics; individual's worldview; civilian versus military component of policy making and policy content); and, (4) external events: act either as a *push* or *pull* factor for Cuba's foreign initiatives. For instance, the regime's decision to develop its Middle Eastern relations in the 1970s came at a time when opportunities for Cuba's activism in its backyard, the Caribbean, and Latin America, were few, and when previous policies had failed. This acted as a *push* factor for a Middle Eastern policy. Similarly, the island modified its activities to accomodate external variables that acted as a *pull* factor away from the Middle East: (1) the Soviet invasion of Afghanistan; (2) the deepening military commitment in Africa; and (3) new opportunities for Cuban policy in Nicaragua, Grenada, El Salvador, and Jamaica, among others.

The relationships between the determinant variables and the outcome (autonomy, converge, or subordination) are the following:

Time. The longer the length of Soviet presence, the greater the degree of Cuban policy subordination to Soviet interests, expecially if the Soviet Union's presence preceeded Cuban presence.

If Cuban presence preceeds the Soviet, the longer the length of Cuban presence, the greater the influence of the Soviet Union on Cuban policy and on the third country. The time progression will lead from relative Cuban autonomy in policy to convergence with the U.S.S.R. and finally to increasing conformity to Soviet interests.

Regime type. In countries whose government is based on a personalistic power base, Cuba will have a greater degree of autonomy; in collective-rule type governments the influence of the Soviet Union will tend to be greater. Consequently, Cuba's policy will tend to be subordinated to the Soviet Union's policy in regimes where there is collective rule.

In non-aligned countries Cuba's autonomy of action will be greater than in Soviet-aligned countries.

Factionalism and bureaucratic politics. There are hard line Marxists and Liberal Marxist factions in the Cuban apparatus. The pro-Soviet faction is headed by Carlos Rafael Rodriguez (the Ministry of Economy) and Raul Castro (the FAR). The Liberal Marxist, Third World-oriented, coalesce around Osmani Cienfuegos and the Ministry of Foreign Relations. The Liberal Marxist tend to promote autonomous policies from Moscow while the hard-line Marxists defend close coordination with Soviet policy.

Other major cleavages within the Cuban apparatus appear between civil and military foreign policy bureaucrats.

Military personnel tend to be closely aligned and subordinated to Soviet Policy. Civilian elites, if working for the Ministry of Foreign Relations or under Isidoro Malmierca (Organization of Solidarity with the Peoples of Asia, Africa, and Latin America, OSPAAAL) tend to seek autonomy from Soviet policy.

Appendix B
Bibliographic Note

Research on Cuba's relations with Middle Eastern countries (with the minor exception of Cuban-Israeli relations) is non-existent. The researcher, therefore, must make his or her own path as he or she goes along. First, bibliographies on Cuba (published both in and outside the island) are the best place to start to locate primary sources. Among these, the most useful were *Indíce de publicaciones periódicas cubanas*, published by La Biblioteca Jose Marti; Nelson Valdes' *The Cuban Revolution* (especially for documents published by the Foreign Relations Ministry, MINREX, until the 1960s); and, Ronald Chilcote's *Cuba: 1959-1978*. Second, the University of Miami's Cuban Information System provides an invaluable service. The database has indexed periodical articles from *Granma, Bohemia, Verde Olivo*, and *Politica Internacional* (published by the MINREX) from 1980 to 1987. Third, in addition to the ones already mentioned, other Cuban publications such as *Colaboración* and *Revista Tricontinental* are important, although less useful, sources. The monographs, reports, and journals published by the Centro de Estudios de Africa y Medio Oriente in Havana are required reading for anyone interested in Cuba's understanding of Zionism and Islam. Fourth, the Foreign Broadcast Information Service (FBIS) *Latin America* and *Africa and the Middle East* are essential sources for tracing day to day contact between the island and Middle Eastern countries. The *Cuban Chronology* published by the U.S. government is also very helpful in this regard. Trade statistics are available in Cuba's *Anuario estadistico* and in the U.N. *Trade Yearbook*. Finally, for the Middle East side of the equation, the *Mid-East File* and the FBIS are worthwhile sources. *Al Ahram*, the major Egyptian newspaper, did not provide much information on the topic.

This bibliographic note does not pretend to be exhaustive. Other traditional avenues of research are available (i.e., international and U.S. press agencies, secondary sources, and U.S. government documents) and should be consulted.

Appendix C
An Overview of Middle Eastern Countries

BAHRAIN
(State of Bahrain)

Area: 240 sq. mi.; 633 sq. km.
Population: 400,000 (1985E)
Per Capita GNP: US $10,510
Official language: Arabic

Bahrain achieved its independence in 1971 after attempts
to form a federation with the UAE and Qatar failed. Although
Bahrain adopted a constitution in 1973 that guarantees its
citizens many democratic rights, representation in governmental
decision making is not included. The Amir is the head of state
and the traditional ruler. He has an appointed Council of
Ministers called the Cabinet who advise him on different
concerns. Many are also members of the royal family. A
National assembly was formed with the adoption of the
constitution in 1973, but it was dissolved in 1975 by an Amiri
decree. Political parties are illegal. Sheikh Khalifa Bin Sulman
al Khalifa has reigned as Amir since 1971.

EGYPT
(Arab Republic of Egypt)

Area: 386,659 sq. mi.; 1,001,449 sq. km.
Population: 48,489,000 (1985E)
Per Capita GNP: US $700 (1983)
Official Language: Arabic

135

Egypt was under British mandate until 1922, when it was granted independence. British influence, however, remained strong in Egypt. The British military force controlled the Suez Canal until 1956 when it became nationalized. Egyptian monarchy ended in 1952 when King Farouk was overthrown in a coup led by a faction of the military command called the "Free Officers" which included two of Egypt's future leaders: Col. Gamal Abdel Nasser and Col. Anwar Sadat. Nasser became a national and international leader who sought non-alignment while establishing cloer relations with the USSR. After Nasser's death, Sadat assumed power. He shifted Egypt's international relations away from Moscow closer to Washington. In 1981, President Sadat was assasinated by Muslim emtremists and succeeded by Muhammad Hosni Mubarak, also a military man. Overall, Mubarak has continued Sadat's international course. Under the present government, executive power is held by a president nominated by the legislature and elected by popular vote to a six-year term. Vice-presidents and ministers are appointed by the president. The People's Assembly is a unicameral legislative body consisting of 250 members elected by popular vote.

Diputes with Israel have greatly influence Egyptian politics. Since Israel's formation four wars have broken out. Not until 1979, with the U.S. sponsored Camp David accords, was an Egyptian-Israeli peace treaty negotiated. However, threatned by the still unresolved issue of Palestinian autonomy, this peace is fragile. Egypt under Mubarak continues to have conflicts with Israel, with fundamentalist Muslim movements, and with the radical Arab states.

IRAN
(Islamic Republic of Iran)

Area: 636,293 sq. mi.
Population: 44,073,000 (1985E)
Per Capita GNP: US $2,180 (1977)
Official Language: Persian (Farsi)

Iran was an absolute monarchy under Shah Muhammad Reza Pahlavi until the Islamic revolution in 1979. Despite attempts to modernize his absolute control of political power in Iran, the Shah was overthrown by popular uprisings prompted by the callings of exiled religious leader Ayatollah Ruhollah Khomeini. The constitution adopted in 1979 states that the form of government in Iran is to be an Islamic Republic. The spirituality and ethics of Islam are the basis for political, social, and economic relations, however, other religious believers are provided with equal rights. Iran elects a president for a four-year term, President Sayed Ali Khameni has held office since 1981. Legislative power is held by the Islamic Consultative Assembly, a congress of 270 members elected to four-year terms. Executive, legislative, and judicial branches are subject to the authority of the Wali Faqih, the national religious leader of Iran. The Faqih, currently Ayatollah Khomeini, serves as the supreme authority in the Iranian government. Since 1980, Iran has been at war with Iraq.

IRAQ
(Republic of Iraq)

Area: 167,924 sq. mi.; 434,923 sq. km.
Population: 15,862,000 (1985E)
Per Capita GNP: US $1,530 (1977)
Official Languages: Arabic, Kurdish

Iraq became a republic in 1958 when a group of military officers, led by Brig. Gen. Abdul Karim Kassem, overthrew the government in a coup d'etat. Since then, the Iraqi government has established a socialist state which has close ties to the USSR. Iraqi stability is threatened by the war with Iran since 1980 and growing unrest from the Kurds in the north.

Governmental power in Iraq is held by the President, currently Saddam Hussain, and a Revolutionary Command Council (RCC) consisting of nine members. Legislative duties are the responsibility of both the RCC and a National Assembly of 250 elected members. Routine administration of the country is run by a Council of Ministers. The Iraq Regional Command of the Baath (Arab Socialist) Party also has great influence over the direction of Iraqi politics.

ISRAEL
(State of Israel)

Area: 8,291 sq. mi.; 21,475 sq. km.
Population: 4,255,000 (1985E)
Per Capita GNP: US $5,370 (1983)
Official Languages: Hebrew, Arabic

The State of Israel was formed in a region historically called Palestine, while it was under British Mandate after World

War I. Formation of the Zionist state has created enormous conflict between the Israelis and the neighboring Arab states. The displacement of the Palestinian citizens in 1948 has evolved into a refugee problem that still evades solution. These conflicts erupted into wars with neighboring Arab states in 1948, 1956, 1967, and 1973.

The Israeli government has no constitution, supreme authority rests with the Knesset, an assembly of 120 members elected to four-year terms. A President is elected by the Knesset every five years, and is the constitutional head of state. Executive power lies with the Cabinet, and is led by a Prime Minister. Irael has intimate relations with the U.S. Recently, the Soviets have expressed interest in reestablishing diplomatic relations with Israel.

JORDAN
(Hashemite Kingdom of Jordan)

Area: 37,737 sq. mi.; 97,940 sq. km.
Population: 3,892,000
Per Capita GNP: US $1,640 (1983)
Official Language: Arabic

Jordan was granted independence in 1946 as a constitutional monarchy, ending almost thirty years under British Mandate. King Hussein received the throne in 1951 after the assasination of his grandfather, Abdullah. Legislative power is vested in a bicameral National Assembly. The House of Notables (Senate) has 30 appointed members, and the House of Deputies (Representatives) has 60 members elected to four-year terms. The legislature has the power to override royal vetoes. The King has executive power and is assisted by an appointed Council of Ministers, who are responsible to the assembly. Three of Jordan's territories are currently occupied by Israeli troops, however, Jordan-Israeli relations are not as eruptive as Jewish relations with other neighboring Arab states.

KUWAIT
(State of Kuwait)

Area: 6,880 sq. mi.
Population: 1,983,000 (1985E)
Per Capita GNPDS: US $17,880
Official Language: Arabic

Kuwait is a monarchy with an Amir as head of state. The constitution adopted in 1962 restricts succession to the Amir to heirs of Mubarak al-Sabah. The constitution also guarantees democratic rights to its citizens, including representation in a National Assembly of 50 members. In 1976, after an outbreak of internal unrest, due to the Palestinian problem, the national assembly dissolved. However, in 1981 the National assembly was reestablished and has operated effectively up to the present. The Amir has an appointed council of ministers and a prime minister. It is a power of the Assembly to dismiss a minister and make laws. It is also in the Assembly's jurisdiction to veto decisions of the Amir, however, such rights are rarely pushed. Political parties are legal and participate in the Assembly elections. Sheikh Jabel al Ahmad al-Sabah has been Amir since the death of his cousin in 1977.

LEBANON
(Republic of Lebanon)

Area: 4,015 sq. mi.; 10,400 sq. km.
Population: 3,339,000 (1983E)
Per Capita GNP: US $750 (1977)
Official Language: Arabic (and French)

Lebanon gained its independence as a parlimentary republic in 1941 after almost 25 years under French Mandate. The Lebanese Constitution of 1926 divided the government into a balanced representation of Lebanon's different religious groups. In 1975, the balance collapsed and grew into a civil war. The fighting was heightened when conflict increased between the Palestinian refugees and Israeli troops in 1976. Intervention by Syria, also in 1976, further complicated the conflict. Because the conflict is still destructive toward the re-establishment of political order in Lebanon, it is practically impossible to describe the current political system in Lebanon. Under the 1926 Constitution, legislative responsibility is assigned to a National Assembly of 99 elected members. Representation is proportionally assigned to the major Lebanese religious groups: Maronite Christian, Sunni Muslim, Shiite Muslim, Greek Orthodox Christian, and the Druze. Representation is still based on the populations of each religious group recorded in a 1932 census. A President is elected to a six-year term by the Assembly. The last elections for a National Assembly were held in 1972.

LIBYA
(Socialist People's Libyan Arab Jamahiriya)

Area: 679,358 sq. mi.; 1,759,540 sq. km.
Population: 3,973,000 (1985E)
Per Capita GNP: US $8,480 (1983)
Official Language: Arabic

Twentieth century Libyan politics can be divided into three distinct periods. The first, between 1911 and World War II, when Libya was an Italian colony. The second started in 1957 when Libya gained its independence and became a monarchy under Emir Muhammad Idris al-Senussi. The third period covers the years from 1969 to the present. In 1969, Col. Muammar Qaddafi led a coup d'etat that established the foundations for the revolutionary Socialist republic that governs Libya today.

A constitution adopted in 1977 places the government under the nominal control of a General People's Congress and a General Secretariat. The General People's Congress has representatives from trade unions, professional organizations, the "peoples congresses," and the Revolutionary Command Council. The General Secretariate consists of a General Secretary and three other members. General Secretary, Col. Qaddafi, is also the head of state. Administrative functions are monitored by the General People's Committee. The chairman of this committee also functions as the prime minister. Libya's judicial system includes a People's Court which deals with administrative and political crimes.

Over the past decade, Libya's relations with the United States have declined. Relations with some Middle Eastern and Western states have degenerated as well. The Soviet Union has made tentative advances in the direction of closer ties with the Qaddafi government.

NORTH YEMEN
(Yemen Arab Republic)

Area: 75,290 sq. mi.; 195,000 sq. km.
Population: 8,061,000 (1985E)
Per Capita GNP: US $550 (1983)
Official Language: Arabic

For much of the twentieth century, North Yemen was

inaccessible to Westerners. The government stressed isolation
and enforced policies that made visiting North Yemen very
difficult. Egyptian presence in North Yemen began when
efforts were made to form the United Arab Republic in 1958.
Although the attempt was unsuccessful, Egypt's interest in
North Yemen grew until 1962, when it supported Yemen's new
revolutionary government entrenched in a civil war with Saudi
Arabia--suported royalists. During this period, Egypt had over
70,000 troops stationed in North Yemen. Eventually, the
revolution died and a republic was established.

Today, North Yemen is a republic with a president, vice-
president, and prime minister. These positions are filled by a
Constituent People's Assembly. A General People's Congress
was established in 1982 consisting of 700 elected members and 300
appointed members. The congress meets every two years and
members are re-elected every four years. The current president,
Col. Ali Abdullah Saleh, was elected for a second five-year term
in 1983.

OMAN
(Sultanate of Oman)

Area: 120,000 sq. mi.; 310,800 sq. km.
Population: estimated at over one million citizens
Per Capita GNP: US $2,520 (1977)
Official Language: Arabic

Oman gained its independence in 1951. It is an absolute
monarchy with neither a constitution nor a legislature. The
sultan is the traditional leader; all legislation is by decree. In
1970, Qaboos bin Said, the current Sultan, ousted his father in a
bloodless coup. Sultan Said rules with the advice of an
appointed cabinet and a Consultative Assembly of 55 nominated
members. Political parties are strictly illegal. For many years,
the Dhofar Liberation Front in the southern province of Dhofar
rebelled against the Sultan. The Front received support from
South Yemen, and indirectly from the Soviet Union, East
Germany, and Cuba. The Sultan was supported by Saudi Arabia
and pre-revolutionary Iran. In 1976 a truce was arranged and in
1983 diplomatic relations between South Yemen and Oman
resumed. In 1985, despite close relations with the US, Oman
established diplomatic relations with the USSR.

142

QATAR
(State of Qatar)

Area: 4,247 sq. mi.; 11,000 sq. km.
Population: 142,000 (1985E)
Per Capita GNP: US $21,210 (1983)
Official Language: Arabic

In 1971, after an attempt to join the UAE and Bahrain in a federation failed, Qatar declared its independence as a traditional sheikdom. The head of state is the Amir, his executive power is exercized by an appointed Council of Ministers. Although the governmental structure is very authoritarian, all fundamental democratic rights are guaranteed for citizens of Qatar in a provisional constitution adopted in 1970. An Advisory Council of thirty members, comprised of both elected and appointed members, evaluates legislation. Recently, it was given the power to question individual ministers about propsed legislation before promulgation. Sheikh Khalifa Bin Hamad Al-Thani has been Amir since assuming power in 1972.

SAUDI ARABIA
(Kingdom of Saudi Arabia)

Area: 829,995 sq. mi.; 2,149,690 sq. km.
Population: 10, 864,000 (1985E)
Per Capita GNP: US $12,230 (1983)
Official Language: Arabic

Saudi Arabia was formed in 1932 as an Islamic monarchy under the leadership of the Saud family. The government remains an abosolute monarchy today with neither a legislature nor political parties. Although the Saud royal family has grown into the thousands, political power is consolidated by an inner circle of family members who are future successors to the throne. Almost all of Saudi Arabia's politicval decisions are made by this inner circle. The Saudi King functions also as prime minister and religious leader. Since the late sixties and during the period of economic boom, the royal family has worked at establishing an efficient administrative system.

Saudi Arabia may find its rapid modernization during the seventies and early eighties a threat to its future as a stable, conservative monarchy, especially if royal family quarrels are not resolved. Revolutionary governments in Iran and South Yemen are also a threat to present Saudi security.

SOUTH YEMEN
(People's Democratic Republic of Yemen)

Area: 111,074 sq. mi.; 287,683 sq. km.
Population: 2,291,000 (1985E)
Per Capita GNP: US $520 (1983)
Official Language: Arabic

South Yemen was ruled by Britain first as part of British India, and then as a crown colony until its independence in 1967. British efforts to organize a federation from all of the Yemen tribal groups failed when the National Liberation Front consolidated its power and gained the leadership of South Yemen. Its consitution of 1970 is Marxist-Leninist. Ties with the Soviet Union and Cuba have flourished in the past decade following the signing of a 20-year Treaty of Friendship and Co-operation with the USSR in 1979. This pro-communist stance has worried South Yemen's conservative neighbors and increased tension in the Gulf region.

Legislative power in South Yemen is controlled by the Supreme People's Council, a unicameral body of 111 elected members. The Supreme People's Council elected in December 1978 consists of 71 members of the Yemen Socialist Party and 40 independents. The Supreme People's Council appoints a presidium whose Chairman is the head of state. Politics in South Yemen, however, have been wrought with personalism, factionalism, and violence.

SYRIA
(Syrian Arab Republic)

Area: 71,586 sq. mi.; 185,408 sq. km.
Population: 11,288,000 (1985E)
Per Capita GNP: US $1,760 (1983)
Official Language: Arabic

Since Syria's independence in 1946, Syrian politics has always been tainted with military involvement. The military have had control of the government since 1961, when a military faction of the Baath Party staged a coup d' etat and ended Syria's union attempt with Egypt as a member of the United Arab Republic. In 1971, a group of military officers, led by Lt.

Gen. Hafiz al-Assad seized power, and have retained it ever
since. Assad has served as president since 1972, and was re-
elected for his third seven-year term in 1985. According to the
1973 Constitution, legislative power is vested in a unicameral
People's Council, consisting of 195 elected members. The
president is assisted by a Council of Ministers, led by the Prime
Minister.

Syrian stability is threatened by its continued
involvement in the Lebanon-Israeli crisis, and growing
discontentment with the leadership of the Alawite minority.

UNITED ARAB EMIRATES

Area: 32,278 sq. mi.; 83,600 sq. km.
Population: 1,040,300 (1980C)
Per Capita GNP: US $22,870 (1983)
Official Language: Arabic

The United Arab Emirates gained independence in 1971
after it seceded from a federation with Bahrain and Qatar.
Although internal disputes have tainted relations between the
member emirates, progress toward centralization and federal
control has increased.

The United Arab Emirates is a union of seven territorial
monarchies, each ruled by its hereditary Sultan. The highest
federal authority is the Supreme Council composed of the
leaders of the seven emirates. The Council elects a president
and vice-president from its members. The fully appointed
legislative body, the Federal National Council, has 40 members.
This council considers laws proposed by an appointed Council of
Ministers. Political parties are illegal.

Because Abu Dhabi and Dabai are the only significant
exporters of petroleum, these two emirates dominate UAE
politics.

Sources:

Political Change in the Middle East Sources of Conflict and
   Accommodation, 2nd ed., Prentice Hall Publishers, New
   Jersey, 1987.

The European Yearbook: 1986, Vo. I and II, London: Europe
   Publications, 1986.

Selected Bibliography

A. Periodicals and Journals

Bohemia

Colaboracion

Granma and Granma Weekly Review

Latin American Weekly Report

Politica Internacional

Verde Olivo

B. Information Services

Foreign Broadcast Information Service, *Latin America* (1959-1987) and *Africa and the Middle East* (1959-1987).

C. Articles and Books

Alarcon, Ricardo. "Relaciones entre Cuba y los Estados Unidos: pautas de conducta y opciones." Tokatlian, Juan G., ed. *Cuba-Estados Unidos: dos opciones.* Bogota: CEREC, 1984, pp. 23-30.

Andelman, David A. "Andropov's Middle East." *The Washington Quarterly* 6 (Spring 1983):111-113.

Anti-Defamation League of B'nai B'rith. "P.L.O. Activities in Latin America." New York: Anti-Defamation League, 1982.

146

Baloyra Herp, Enrique. "Internationalism and the Limits of Autonomy: Cuba's Foreign Relations." Muñoz, Heraldo and Joseph S. Tulchin, eds. *Latin American Nations in World Politics*. Boulder: Westview Press, 1983, pp. 168-185.

Bender, Gerald J. "Angola, the Cubans, and American Anxieties." *Foreign Policy* 31 (Spring 1978):3-30.

Benemelis, Juan. "Cuban Leaders and the Soviet Union." Paper presented at the Seminar on Soviet-Cuban Relations in the 1980s, University of Miami, 8 November 1985.

_____. "Cuba's Policy in Africa." (unpubished manuscript).

Blasier, Cole. "The Cuban-U.S.-Soviet Triangle, Changing Angles." *Estudios Cubanos-Cuban Studies* (January 1978).

Campbell, John C. "Soviet Policy in the Middle East." *Current History* 80 (January 1981):1-4, 42-43.

Carrillo, Justo. "Vision and Revision: U.S.-Cuban Relations." *Cuba: Continuity and Change*. Suchlicki, Jaime, Antonio Jorge, and Damián J. Fernández, eds. Miami: University of Miami, 1985.

Cooley, John K. *Libyan Sandstorm: The Complete Account of Qaddafi's Revolution*. New York: Holt, Rinehart and Winston, 1983.

de Rivera, Joseph H. *Psychological Dimensions of Foreign Policy*. Columbus: Charles E. Merrill Publishing Co., 1968.

Defense Intelligence Agency. *Handbook on the Cuban Armed Forces*. (DDB-2680-62-79) Washington: 1979.

Dominguez, Jorge I. "The Armed Forces and Foreign Relations." Mesa-Lago, Carmelo, ed. *Cuba in the World* Pittsburgh: University of Pittsburgh Press, 1978, pp. 53-82.

_____. *Cuba: Order and Revolution*. Cambridge: Harvard University Press, 1975.

_____. "The Cuban Operations in Angola: Costs and Benefits for the Armed Forces." *Cuban Studies-Estudio Cubanos* 1978:10-20.

_____. "Political and Military Limitations and Consequences of Cuban Policies in Africa." Mesa-Lago,

Carmelo and June S. Belkin, eds. *Cuba in Africa*. Pittsburgh: Center for Latin American Studies, 1982, pp. 107-140.

_____. "The Success of Cuban Foreign Policy." Center for Latin American and Caribbean Studies Occasional Papers No. 27. New York: New York University, 1980.

Duncan, W. Raymond. "Funciones de Cuba en el ambito de la comunidad socialista: a la vanguardia de los intereses del Tercer Mundo?" Tokatlián, Juan G. ed. *Cuba-Estados Unidos: dos enfoques*. Bogotá: CEREC, 1984, pp. 77-109.

Durch, William J. "The Cuban Military in Africa and the Middle East: From Algeria to Angola." *Studies in Comparative Communism*. XI (Spring-Summer 1978):34-74.

Eckstein, Susan. "Structural and Ideological Bases of Cuba's Overseas Programs." *Politics and Society*. XXI:95-121.

The Economist Foreign Report. "Castro's First Middle East Adventure: Part II." 15 March 1978, pp. 5-6.

English, Adrian J. "The Cuban Revolutionary Armed Forces." Janes Defence Weekly, (June 30, 1984):1066-73.

Eran, Oded. "Soviet Middle East Policy: 1967-1973." Rabinovich, Itamar and Haim Shaked, eds. *From June to October: The Middle East Between 1967 and 1973*. New Brunswick: Transaction Books, 1978, pp. 25-50.

Erisman, H. Michael. *Cuba's International Relations: The Anatomy of a Nationalistic Foreign Policy*. Boulder: Westivew, 1985.

Falk, Pamela S. *Cuban Foreign Policy: Caribbean Tempest*. Lexington: D.C. Heath, 1986.

Fauriol, Georges A. *Foreign Policy Behavior of Caribbean States: Guyana, Haiti, and Jamaica*. Lanham: United Press of America, 1984.

Franqui, Carlos. *Family Portrait with Fidel: A Memoir*. New York: Random House, 1984.

Frechette, Myles R.R. "Cuba en los ochentas." Tokatlián, Juan G., ed. *Cuba-Estados Unidos: dos enfoques*. Bogotá: CEREC, 1984, pp. 45-58.

Furtak, Robert K. "Cuba: analisis." Drekonya, Gerhard K. and Juan G. Tokatlián, eds. *Teoría y práctica de la política exterior latinoamericana.* Bogotá: Universidad de los Andes, 1983, pp. 461-88.

_____. "Cuba: un cuarto de siglo de política exterior revolucionaria." *Foro Internacional.* XXV, (April-June 1985):343-361.

Gonzalez, Edward. "After Fidel: Political Succession in Cuba." *Problems of succession in Cuba.* Miami: University of Miami, 1985, pp. 3-19.

_____. "Complexities of Cuban Foreign Policy." *Problems of Communism.* (November-December 1977):1-15.

Judson, Fred. *Cuba and the REvolutionary Myth: The Political Education of the Rebel Army, 1953-68.* Boulder: Westview Press, 1984.

Karol, K.S. *Guerrillas in Power.* London: Jonathan Cape, 1971.

Legum, Colin and Haim Shaked, eds. *The Middle East Contemporary Survey.* Vols. I-III. New York: Holmes and Meir, 1977-1980.

LeoGrande, William M. "Civil-Military Relations in Cuba: Party Control and Political Socialization." *Studies in Comparative Communism,* Autumn 1978, p. 278-91.

_____. "Cuban-Soviet Relations and Cuban Policy in Africa." Mesa-lago, Carmelo and June S. Belkin, eds. *Cuba in Africa.* Pittsburgh: University of Pittsburgh Press, 1982, pp. 13-49.

Levine, Barry, ed. *The New Cuban Presence in the Caribbean.* Boulder: Westview, 1983.

Lutwak, Edward. "Cubans in Arabia? Or the Meaning of Strategy." *Commentary* 68 (December 1979): 62-66.

Martínez Salsamendi, Carlos. "Cuba en América Central, el Caribe y Africa." Tokatlián, Juan G., ed. *Cuba-Estados Unidos: dos enfoques.* Bogotá: CEREC, 1984, 127-198.

McColm, Bruce R. "Central America and the Caribbean: The Larger Scenario." *Strategic Review.* (Summer 1983).

McShane, John. "Cuban Foreign Policy: Global Orientations." *Latinamericanist.* 14 (31 May 1979):1-4.

Mesa-Lago, Carmelo. "Cuban Foreign Policy in Africa: A General Framework." Mesa-Lago, Carmelo and June S. Belkin, eds. *Cuba in Africa.* Pittsburgh: University of Pittsburgh Press, 1982, pp. 3-12.

Mesa-Lago, Carmelo and June S. Belkin, eds. *Cuba in Africa.* Pittsburgh: University of Pittsburgh Press, 1982.

The Middle East and North Africa. London: Europe Publications, 1969-1982.

Nation, R. Craig. "The Sources of Soviet Involvement in the Middle East." Kauppi, Mark V. and R. Craig Nations, eds. *The Soviet Union and the Middle East in the 1980s.* Lexington: Lexington Books, 1983, pp. 41-70.

Nolan, David. *FSLN: The Ideology of the Sandinistas and the Nicaraguan Revolution.* Miami: University of Miami, 1984.

Perez-Lopez, Jorge F. "The 1982 Cuban Joint Venture Law: Context, Assessments, and Prospects." Miami: University of Miami, 1985.

Queiser Morales, Waltraud. "Motivations of Cuban Military Internationalism." Paper presented at the 1979 Convention of the Latin American Studies Association: Bloomington, Indiana.

"Relations Between the Palestinian Terrorists and Cuba." Reprinted from *PLO in Lebanon: Selected Documents.* Israeli, Raphael, ed. London: Weindenfeld and Nicolson, 1983, pp. 144-58.

Reydnolds, P.A. *An Introduction to International Relations.* Cambridge: Schenkman Publishing Co., 1971.

Rosenau, James N. "El pluralista empirico vs. los puntos de vista de las grandes teorias sobre relaciones internacionales (actores, niveles y sistemas)." *Foro Internacional.* XXV, (April-June 1985):301-310.

_____. *International Politics and Foreign Policy.* New York: Free Press, 1969.

150

Roumani, Jacques. "From Republic to Jamahiriya: Libya's Search for Political Community." *The Middle East Journal.* 37 (Spring 1983):151-168.

Rubinstein, Alvin Z. "The Soviet Presence in the Arab World." *Current History* 80 (OCtober 1981):313-318.

Saddy, Fehmy, ed. *Arab-Latin American Relations: Energy, Trade, and Investment.* New Brunswick: Transaction Books, 1983.

Shapira, Yoram. "Cuba and the Arab-Israeli Conflict." Mesalago, Carmelo and Cole Blasier, eds. *Cuba in the World.* Pittsburgh: University of Pittsburgh Press, 1979, pp. 153-166.

Siljander, Mark. "The Palestine Liberation Organization in Central America." Mimeo. October 1983.

Smoke, Richard and Alexander L. George. *Deferrence in American Foreign Policy: Theory and Practice.* New York: Columbia University Press, 1974.

Suarez, Andres. "Civil Military Relations in Cuba." Paper presented at the seminar on the Cuban Armed Forces, University of Miami, August 16, 1985.

_____. "Cuba: Ideology and Pragmatism." Suchlicki, Jaime, Antonio Jorge, and Damián J. Fernández, eds. *Cuba: Continuity and Change.* Miami: University of Miami, 1986.

Suchlicki, Jaime. "Is Castro Ready to Accommodate?" *Strategic Review.* (Spring 1984):22-29.

Suchlicki, Jaime, Antonio Jorge, and Damián J. Fernández, eds. *Cuba: Continuity and Change.* Miami: University of Miami, 1986.

Tokatlián, Juan G. *Cuba-Estados Unidos: dos enfoques.* Bogotá: CEREC, 1984.

Tretiak, Daniel. *Perspectives on Cuba's Relations with the Communist System: The Politics of a Communist Independent, 1959-1969.* Ann Arbor: Xerox University Microfilms, 1975.

United States Department of State. "Cuban Armed Forces and the Soviet Military Presence." Department of State Bulletin (September 1982):64-68.

_____. "The Sandinistas and the Middle Eastern Radicals."
    Washington, D.C.: Department of State, August 1985.

United States Government. *Libya: A Country Study.* Washington:
    Government Printing Office, 1979.

Valdes, Nelson P. "The Evolution of Cuban Foreign Policy in
    Africa." Paper presented at the 1979 International Studies
    Association Meeting, Toronto, Canda.

Vellinga, M.L. "The Military and Dynamics of the Cuban
    Revolutionary Process." *Comparative Politics* (January
    1976):245-270.

Viotti, Paul R. "Politics in the Yemens and the Horn of Africa:
    Constraints on a Super Power." Mark V. Kauppi and R.
    Craig Nations, eds. *The Soviet Union and the Middle East in the
    1980s.* Lexington: D.C. Heath, 1983.

White House Office of Media Relations. "The PLO in Central
    America." *The White House Digest.* 20 July 1983.

Wright, John L. *Libya: A Modern History.* Baltimore: The Johns
    Hopkins University Press, 1982.

Yodfat, Aryeh Y. *The Soviet Union and the Arabian Peninsula.*
    London: Croom Helm, 1983.

Index

AALAPSO. *See* Afro-Asian–Latin
American Peoples' Solidarity
Organization
Addis Ababa, Ethiopia, 54
Aden, South Yemen, 22, 47, 116
Aden Pact, 67
Afghanistan, 13–14, 46, 85, 109, 119,
122, 125
Africa, 12–13, 15, 17, 24–25, 29, 45, 48
military cooperation, 9–11, 55, 57, 77,
106, 120, 124
See also individual countries
Afro-Asian–Latin American Peoples'
Solidarity Organization (AALAPSO
or OSPAAL), 90
Alarcon, Ricardo, 39
Algeria, 4, 38
ideology, 71, 79–81, 116
military cooperation, 1, 9, 11, 36–37,
43, 55, 79–80, 124
socio-economic cooperation, 11, 61,
79–81, 122
See also Algiers, Algeria
Algerian Front for National Liberation
(FNL), 43, 80
Algiers, Algeria, 10, 45, 72, 102
Allende, Salvador, 11–12, 27
Andelman, David, 121
Angola, 26
and Cuban prestige, 3, 7, 46, 106,
125
ideology, 16, 24–25, 71
military cooperation, 1, 11–12, 57,
66–67, 77, 103, 120–121, 124
Soviet relations, 11, 18, 70
Anti-Americanism. *See under* United
States of America

Anti-Defamation League of B'nai B'rith,
74
Antigua, 14
Arab countries. *See* Middle East
Arab-Israeli War (1967), 3, 38–39. *See
also* Israel, Arab conflict
Arab Socialist Baath Party, 77, 83
Arab Union of Cuba, 57
Arafat, Yasser, 47–48, 72–75, 78–79,
122
ARC. *See* Revolutionary Army of the
Caribbean
Argentina, 9, 14, 22, 28, 104
Assad, Hafiz Al-, 75, 78, 122
Association for Syrian-Cuban Friendship,
78
Asylum issue, 14
Athir Medal of the National Merit Order,
81
'Aysani, Shibila Al-, 83
Azizi, Ahmad, 87

Baath Party. See Arab Socialist Baath
Party
Bahrain, 92–93, 124
Baloyra, Enrique, 20, 22
Batista, Fulgencio, 42, 44
Bay of Pigs, 10
Ben Bella, Ahmed, 80
Bendjedid, Chaddi, 81
Benemelis, Juan, 25, 55, 57
Bilal, Muhain, 76
Bishop, Maurice, 36, 111
Black September (PLO faction), 74–75
Blasier, Cole, 9
Bohemia, 72, 103
Bolivia, 9

154

Brazil, 9, 104
Brezhnev, Leonid, 106
Bridge linkages. *See under* Cuban foreign
     policy
Briqadistas, 57, 82, 92, 109
Burnham, Linden Forbes Sampson, 83

Cambras, Rodrigo Alvarez, 82
Camp David Accords (1978), 41, 53–54,
     71, 89
Cancun, Mexico, 14
Caribbean Basin, 12, 14–15, 49, 111.
     See also individual countries
Carter, Jimmy, 13
Carter Doctrine, 41
Castro, Fidel, 44, 75, 83–84, 88, 90
     aspirations, 11, 15–16, 39, 51, 54, 80,
          99–100, 106, 126–127
     decision-making role, 22, 24–25, 51,
          57, 117
     ideology, 8–9, 12, 16–17, 20–21, 23,
          36, 86, 89, 116–117
     international travel, 10, 13, 45–46, 81,
          103
     leadership aspirations, 11, 15–16, 39,
          51, 54, 80, 99–100, 106, 126–127
     líder máximo, 11–12, 17, 22–23, 26,
          36, 117
     relations with Qaddafi, 101–104,
          106–107, 111
     on religion, 86–87
Castro, Raul, 77
Castroism, 2. *See also* Castro, Fidel,
     ideology
Castro Ruz, Ramon, 67
CCW. *See* Central of Cuban Workers
CDR. *See* Committees for the Defense
     of the Revolution
Central America. *See* Latin America
Central Intelligence Agency (U.S.), 103
Central of Cuban Workers (CCW), 83
Chernenko, Konstantin, 72
Chile, 9, 11–12, 27, 104
China. *See* People's Republic of China
Cienfuegos, Osmani, 22, 25, 55, 57, 69
Colombia, 9, 11, 15
COMECON. *See* Council for Mutual
     Economic Assistance
Committees for the Defense of the
     Revolution (CDR), 66, 83

Communism, 9, 22, 37, 49, 53, 57,
     118–119. *See also* Marxism-
     Leninism
Conference of Solidarity with the Peoples
     of Africa, Asia, and Latin America
     (1966), 9
Confrontation Front states, 71, 124
Congo, 9
Convergence theory. *See* Cuban foreign
     policy, dependence, convergence,
     independence theories
Costa Rica, 15, 104
Council for Mutual Economic Assistance
     (COMECON), 10
Cuban-Arab Friendship Committee, 57
Cuban Communist Party (PCC), 10–11,
     75, 77, 83
     decision-making role, 13, 25, 43, 117
     ideology, 19–20, 48–49, 68, 73
Cuban Constitution, 19
Cuban Council of Ministers, 12
Cuban Council of State, 12, 20
Cuban foreign policy, 19
     active internationalism (1975–1980),
          11–14
     Africa, 3–4, 9, 15, 17, 25, 48, 79–81,
          88
     bridge linkages, 55, 110–111, 125
     decision-making establishment, 16–17,
          22, 24–26, 51–52, 70, 120
     dependence, convergence, independence
          theories, 1–2, 7, 17–18, 22–23, 41,
          69, 117, 122–123
     diplomatic efforts, 12, 15–16, 26–27,
          38, 55, 67–68, 77–78, 85, 91–92,
          100–107, 110–112, 116, 127
     domestic implications, 2, 22, 24–26,
          35, 103, 118–119, 122–124
     framework for analysis, 129–131
     increasing internationalism
          (1968–1974), 10–11
     initial period (1959–1967), 8–10
     Latin America, 7–9, 14–15, 21, 27–29
     military internationalism
          (1973–present), 75
     new internationalism (late 1980s),
          15–16
     non-alignment, 14, 17, 23, 26, 35, 45,
          52, 71, 78–79, 99, 102, 116
     restrained internationalism (1980–mid-

1980s), 14–16
and revolutionary movements, 2, 9, 16, 23, 27, 111
See also individual countries; Middle East policy; Military cooperation; Socio-economic cooperation
Cuban General Directorate of Investigation (DGI), 25–26
Cuban Ministry of Construction Abroad, 26, 117
Cuban Ministry of Foreign Relations, 24–25, 36, 42, 47, 57, 78, 125
Cuban Ministry of the Revolutionary Armed Forces (MINFAR), 12
Cuban Missile Crisis (1962), 9
Cuban National Assembly of the Peoples Power, 77
Cuban revolution, 8–9, 22, 27, 29, 36, 88
Cuban-Syrian Friendship Committee, 57
Cuban-Syrian Joint Inter-Governmental Commission for Economic and Scientific Cooperation, 78
Czechoslovakia, 9–10, 102

Democratic Front for the Liberation of Palestine, 74
Dependencia theory, 23. *See also* Cuban foreign policy, dependence, convergence, independence theories
Detente, 50
Development assistance. *See* Socio-economic cooperation
DGI. *See* Cuban General Directorate of Investigation
Dhofar region, 57, 66–67, 92–93
Diplomacy. *See* Cuban foreign policy, diplomatic efforts
Dirección General de Investigación. *See* Cuban General Directorate of Investigation
Dominguez, Jorge, 10, 18, 27
Dorticos, Osvaldo, 89
Durch, William J., 82

Eastern Europe, 10, 17, 50, 108, 121
Eckstein, Susan, 28
Economic cooperation. *See* Socio-economic cooperation
Ecuador, 15

Egypt, 4, 37, 103
Israeli relations, 41, 50, 53, 89
Libyan relations, 105
military cooperation, 89
socio-economic cooperation, 61, 88–90
Soviet relations, 50–52, 89–90, 105, 119–120
U.S. relations, 105, 115, 119
El Salvador, 14, 21, 28–29, 35, 68, 109–111
Equatorial Guinea, 11
Erisman, H. Michael, 13, 53, 84
Eritrea, 45, 106
Espinosa Martin, Ramon, 104
Espionage. *See* Intelligence and security
Estrada, Ulises, 47
Ethiopia, 7, 28, 125
Libyan relations, 106, 110
military cooperation, 1, 3–4, 12–13, 25, 46, 55, 57, 67, 77, 120–121, 124
socio-economic cooperation, 25, 45, 67, 88
Somali relations, 12–13, 45, 88, 106, 116
Soviet relations, 11, 18, 24
Ethnicity, 24, 37
Europe, 10, 12, 17, 50, 108, 119, 121

Falklands-Malvinas war, 14, 28
FAR. *See* Revolutionary Armed Forces
Farah, Levi, 57, 73, 77, 79
Fatah, Al (PLO faction), 47, 73, 79
FCW. *See* Federation of Cuban Women
Federation of Cuban Women (FCW), 83
Fez Peace Plan, 122
FNL. *See* Algerian Front for National Liberation
Ford, Gerald R., 13
Foreign debt crisis, 15, 21, 27, 81, 126
France, colonialism, 80, 111
Franco, Francisco, 27
Frank Pais Orthopedic Hospital, 82
French Guyana, 111
Frente Sandinista de Liberacion Nacional. *See* Sandinista Front for National Liberation
Friendship Committees, 57
FSLN. *See* Sandinista Front for National Liberation

156

Fuerzas Armadas Revolucionarias. See Revolutionary Armed Forces

Ghana, 28
Golan Heights, 55
Gonzalez, Edward, 18
Great Britain, colonialism, 65, 92
Grenada, 7, 11–12, 14–15, 28, 36, 109–111, 117, 123, 125
Group of 77, 27
Guadeloupe, 111
Guatemala, 9
Guerrilla movements, 4, 8–9, 15–17, 29, 37, 44, 49, 57, 72–75, 107, 110–111. *See also* Military cooperation
Guevara, Ernesto "Che," 1, 9–10, 80
Guyana, 12, 83, 110

Habash, George, 47–48, 73, 75
Haivi, George, 92
Harvatimah, Nayib, 73
Hasani, Ali Nasir Muhammed Al-, 68–69
"Health for Everyone: 25 Years of Cuban Experience" (conference), 82
Hernandez, Melba, 90
Horn of Africa, 67
Hungary, 102
Hurricane Frederick (1979), 83
Husayn, Ahmad, 83
Hussein (king of Jordan), 83, 90, 121

Ibrahim, Ahman Taleb, 81
Ideology, 16–17, 22, 49
  vs. pragmatism, 35–37, 39, 41–42, 115–117
  See also Imperialism; Marxism-Leninism; Proletarian internationalism; United States of America, anti-Americanism
Imperatorio Grave de Peralta, Julio, 94
Imperialism, 9–10, 15–16, 19, 37, 40–41, 44, 49, 54, 71, 73–76, 89, 103–104, 119
Independence theory. *See* Cuban foreign policy, dependence, convergence, independence theories
India, 83, 87
Intelligence and security, 25–26, 108
International brigadeers, 57, 82, 92, 109

International Conference of Solidarity with the Struggles of the African and Arab Peoples Against Imperialism and Reaction (1978), 54
International Cultural Congress (1968), 44
International lobbying efforts, 22, 27–28, 54, 69, 72, 88
International mediation, 35–36, 119
  in the Middle East, 40, 47–48, 50, 52–54, 70, 73–74, 78–79, 83–85, 87–88, 90, 93–94, 100, 116, 121–122, 124–125
  organizational forums, 4, 20, 27–28, 39–40, 43–45, 51, 76, 85, 100, 116
  See also International lobbying
IPP. *See* Iranian People's Party
Iran, 4, 41, 73, 93
  ideology, 85–88, 116
  Iraqi relations, 3, 37, 46, 50, 52, 83–84, 87–88, 118
  socio-economic cooperation, 61, 85–88
Iranian People's Party (IPP), 85–86, 88
Iranian Revolution (1979), 85–86
Iraq, 4, 57, 106
  ideology, 116, 118
  Iranian relations, 3, 37, 46, 50, 52, 83–84, 87–88, 118
  military cooperation, 11, 45, 55, 74, 82, 124
  socio-economic cooperation, 11, 61, 82–85, 125–126
  Soviet relations, 84–85, 121–122
  U.S. relations, 119, 121–122
Islam, 41, 52, 88, 100, 119
Ismail, Abdal-Fattah, 67
Israel, 1, 68
  Arab conflict, 3, 37–45, 50, 53–54, 71–72, 75–77, 89–92, 115, 124–125
  Libyan relations, 100–101, 104–105, 107, 109
  Soviet relations, 38–45, 50–51, 89, 116, 118
  U.S. relations, 4, 41, 44, 47–50, 71–72, 118
Israeli Defense Forces, 72
Israeli-Egyptian war (1967), 89

Jallud, Abdel Salam, 107

Jamahiriya, 104
Jamaica, 12, 14, 104
Japanese Red Army, 110
Jordan, 4, 37, 90–91, 119, 121
July 26 Movement, 43

Kampuchea, 14
Karol, K.S., 44
Kennedy, John F., 9
KGB (Soviet intelligence), 26
Khomeini, Ruhollah (Ayatollah), 86–88, 121
Khruschev, Nikita, 9
Kuwait, 4, 37, 45, 54, 90–91, 93, 118–119

Labor exportation, 11–12, 55, 66–68, 91, 107–108, 124
domestic implications, 2, 22, 122–123
internationalist duty, 109
Latin America, 4, 8–9, 11, 14–15, 27, 38, 45, 68
Middle East relations, 54–55, 74, 83, 88, 100, 104–106, 110–112, 125
revolutionary movements, 17, 29, 86, 100–101
See also individual countries
LCP. *See* Lebanese Communist Party
Lebanese Communist Party (LCP), 4, 37, 68, 92
Lebanese National Movement, 92
Lebanon, 37, 42, 53, 61, 68, 72–74, 90–92, 118, 121
Liberation theology, 15, 86
Libya, 4, 37, 46, 71, 122
foreign policy objectives, 99–101
ideology, 99, 106, 116, 118
Israeli relations, 100–101, 104, 107, 109
Latin American relations, 100, 104–105, 110–112, 125
Middle East relations, 103, 105–106, 111–112
military cooperation, 29, 74, 108, 124
socio-economic cooperation, 67, 104, 125
Soviet relations, 99–101, 105–106, 108–109, 112
U.S. relations, 100–103, 107, 109–112

Libyan Arab-Cuban Economic and Social Cooperation Commission, 107

McShane, John, 11
Malmierca, Isidoro, 57, 84, 87
Malvinas, 14, 22, 28
Mariam, Mengistu Haile, 13
Martinique, 111
Marxism-Leninism, 9, 41
Arab opposition, 75, 86, 93, 106, 118–119
and Castroism compared, 16, 20, 23, 86
See also Communism
Marxist Popular Movement for the Liberation of Angola (MPLA), 12, 71
Medal of Solidarity, 67
Mesa-Lago, Carmelo, 129
Mexico, 9, 12, 14, 104, 126
Middle East
Arab factionalism, 2, 35–36, 47, 116, 118–120
ideology, 41, 53, 116, 118–119
Latin American relations, 54–55, 74, 83, 88, 100, 104–106, 110–112, 125
See also Middle East policy
Middle East policy, 1, 9, 11, 16
accommodation to the Soviet line (1973–1977), 44–45
activism and role expansion (1977–1980), 45–46
autonomy-dual policy (1959–1973), 42–44
domestic implications and prospects, 3, 117–120, 124–127
historical background, 36–42
ideological and pragmatic principles, 2, 17, 21, 35–37, 39, 41–42, 47, 57, 80, 115–117
mediation, 42, 47–48, 50, 52–54, 124–125
moderate activism (1981–1985), 46
new internationalism (1985–1987), 47–48
and oil needs, 39–41, 126
overview of relations, 56 (table)
strategy, 35–36, 55, 57
See also individual countries

158

Military cooperation, 12, 16, 46, 54, 116, 118, 126
  domestic implications, 123–124
  and Soviet equipment, 4, 44–45, 55, 66, 108, 112, 120–122, 124
  See also Guerrilla movements; *See also under individual countries*
MINFAR. *See* Cuban Ministry of the Revolutionary Armed Forces
Morente Caballero, Jorge, 93–94
Morocco, 43, 80–81
Mozambique, 11
MPLA. *See* Marxist Popular Movement for the Liberation of Angola
Mubarak, Hosni, 89–90, 120

NAM. See Non-Aligned Movement
Nasser, Gamal Abdel, 44, 50–51, 58, 88–89, 102, 119
National Liberation Front (NLF), 65–66
National Liberation Front of Bahrain (NLFB), 93
Neto, Agostinho, 12
Neutrality. *See* Cuban foreign policy, non-alignment
New International Economic Order (NIEO), 27–28, 81, 99
Nicaragua, 9, 12, 14, 21, 28–29, 55, 109, 125
  Middle East relations, 71, 74, 88, 93, 100, 104, 106, 110
  See also Sandinista Front for National Liberation
NIEO. *See* New International Economic Order
NLF. *See* National Liberation Front
NLFB. *See* National Liberation Front of Bahrain
Nolan, David, 29
Non-Aligned Movement (NAM), 3–4, 10, 12, 116, 125
  on the Arab-Israeli conflict, 39–40, 42, 45, 53, 72
  Cuban-Libyan friction, 46, 51, 100, 102, 105–106
  Middle East participation, 76, 78, 81, 83, 85, 87–88, 90
North Africa, 74
North America. *See individual countries*
North Korea, 29

North-South Conference at Cancun (1981), 14
North Vietnam, 29
North Yemen. *See* Yemen Arab Republic

OAS. *See* Organization of American States
October War (1973), 45, 76–77, 105
Ogaden region, 13, 45
Oil supplies, 36, 39–41, 45, 58, 122, 126
  exploration, 67, 93
  and Libya, 104–106, 111
Oman, 37, 57, 66–68, 92–93, 115, 124
OPEC. *See* Organization of Petroleum Exporting Countries
Order of Courage, 104
Organization of American States (OAS), 8, 11
Organization of Petroleum Exporting Countries (OPEC), 3, 37, 39–40, 45, 105, 126
Oropesa, Jesus Montane, 57, 75
Ortega, Daniel, 83
OSPAAL. *See* Afro-Asian–Latin American Peoples' Solidarity Organization

Palestine Liberation Organization (PLO), 4, 41, 43, 80–81, 87, 91–92, 101, 106, 110, 116
  factionalism, 3, 47–48, 72–75, 78, 100, 118, 122, 125
  military cooperation, 44, 72–73
  See also Palestinian rights
Palestinian rights, 28, 37–39, 41, 49, 57, 68, 89. *See also* Palestine Liberation Organization
Panama, 11–12, 15, 27, 104
Panama Canal, 27
Partido Socialista Popular (PSP), 43
PCC. *See* Cuban Communist Party
PDFLP. *See* Popular Democratic Front for the Liberation of Palestine
PDRY. *See* People's Democratic Republic of Yemen
People's Democratic Republic of Yemen (PDRY), 4, 22, 37, 52, 58, 92, 120
  factionalism, 47, 69–70, 118

ideology, 68, 116
Libyan relations, 106, 110
military cooperation, 11, 45, 55,
    66–67, 74, 124
socio-economic cooperation, 11, 61,
    67–68, 93, 125
Soviet relations, 25, 47, 65–66, 68–69
People's Militia, 82
People's Republic of China, 9, 58, 122
Persian Gulf, 40–41, 82–84, 88, 121
Peru, 9, 11, 15
PF. *See* Polisaria Front
PFLO. *See* Popular Front for the
    Liberation of Oman
PFLP. *See* Popular Front for the
    Liberation of Palestine
PLO. *See* Palestine Liberation
    Organization
Pointe Salines airport (Grenada), 111
Poland, 122
Polisario Front (PF), 4, 80–81
Popular Democratic Front for the
    Liberation of Palestine (PDFLP),
    73
Popular Front for the Liberation of
    Oman, (PFLO), 37, 92–93
Popular Front for the Liberation of
    Palestine (PFLP), 47, 73, 75
Proletarian internationalism, 2, 17, 21,
    37, 57, 80
PSP. *See Partido Socialista Popular*
Puerto Rico, 27, 83

Qaddafi, Muammar, 45–46, 51, 54, 88,
    99–104, 106–108, 111
Qaddumi, Faruq, 71

Reagan, Ronald, 14, 21, 46, 109, 126
Regueiro, Julio Cesar, 68
Revolutionary Armed Forces (FAR),
    12–13, 55, 121, 126
decision-making role, 24–25, 57, 117
international military missions, 15,
    29, 45, 67–68, 123–124
Revolutionary Army of the Caribbean
    (ARC), 111
Revolutionary Coordinating Junta, 101,
    110
Roa, Raul, 40
Robaya Ali, Salem, 67, 69

Rodriguez, Carlos Rafael, 25, 57, 69,
    83–84, 103
Romero, Napoleon, 29
Ronfeldt, David, 18
Rosales del Toro, Ulises, 104
Rubinstein, Alvin Z., 49

Sadat, Anwar, 50, 53, 89–90, 115
St. Kitts-Nevis, 14
St. Lucia, 14
St. Vincent, 14
Salsamendi, Carlos Martinez, 20, 28
Sandinista Front for National Liberation
    (FSLN), 14, 21, 29, 35, 55, 68, 71,
    74, 100, 104
Saudi Arabia, 41, 54, 61, 67–68, 93,
    115, 119, 121
Scholarship programs. *See under* Socio-
    economic cooperation
Second Declaration of Havana (1962), 20
Security. *See* Intelligence and security
September revolution (1969), 101
Shapira, Yoram, 43, 103
Sierra Leone, 11
Six Day War (1967), 50
Socio-economic cooperation, 25, 45–46,
    54, 68, 75–76, 78–81, 83–85,
    88–89, 92, 94, 108–109, 116
and domestic issues, 122–125
and foreign policy, 11, 28
scholarship programs, 28–29, 67,
    72–73, 107
trade relations, 55, 57–58, 59–60
    (tables), 61, 77, 82, 93, 101, 104,
    107–109, 125–126
Somalia, 11–13, 45, 88, 116
Somoza, Anastasio, 14, 21, 74
South Africa, 71, 109
South America. *See* Latin America
South Yemen. *See* People's Democratic
    Republic of Yemen
Spain, 27, 58
Steadfastness and Confrontation Front
    states, 71, 124
Strait of Hormuz, 93
Suarez, Andres, 16, 117
Subirana y Lobo, Richard, 43
Suriname, 110, 111
Syrian Arab Republic, 4, 37, 71, 73
ideology, 75–76, 116, 118

160

Middle East relations, 45, 76–78, 105–106, 110
military cooperation, 11, 29, 45, 55, 75–77, 124
socio-economic cooperation, 11, 61, 75–76, 78–79, 116
Soviet relations, 75, 121
U.S. relations, 75–76, 78, 119
Syrian Foreign Ministry, 78
Syrian People's Assembly, 76–77

Tercermundismo (pro–Third World politics), 109
Terrorist organizations, 4, 49. *See also* Guerrilla movements
Third World countries, 4, 9–14, 21, 23–24, 68. *See also individual countries*
Trade relations. *See under* Socio-economic cooperation
Tricontinental Conference of Solidarity of Peoples (1966), 27, 38–39, 44, 65–66
Trinidad-Tobago, 12
Tunis, Tunisia, 72, 108
Tupamaros, 110

UJC. *See* Union of Communist Youth
UNECA. *See* Caribbean Construction Enterprises
Unión Nacional de Empresas del Caribe. *See* Union of Caribbean Construction Enterprises
Union of Caribbean Construction Enterprises (UNECA), 26, 107
Union of Communist Youth (UJC), 83
Union of Soviet Socialist Republics (U.S.S.R.), 3, 26, 61, 106, 110
active internationalism phase (1975–1980), 11–13
dependence, convergence, independence theories, 1–2, 7, 17–18, 22–23, 41, 69, 117, 122–123
framework for analysis, 120–131
ideology, 12, 19–20
increasing internationalism phase (1968–1974), 10–11
the initial period (1959–1967), 9–10
invasion of Afghanistan, 14, 46, 85, 119, 122, 125

Libyan relations, 99–101, 105–106, 108–109, 112
Middle East relations, 1–2, 10, 24, 36, 38–43, 45, 48–54, 70, 84, 89–90, 102, 116, 118–122
military cooperation, 4, 44–45, 54–55, 74, 108, 112, 120–122
U.S. relations, 49, 122
United Nations, 4, 20, 27, 43–44, 54, 72, 88, 92, 100, 125
United Nations Decolonization Committee, 83
United Nations General Assembly, 14
United Nations Security Council, 3, 14
United States of America (U.S.A.) 1, 4, 9–10, 13–15, 26–27, 29, 47, 68, 100–101, 124
anti-Americanism, 8, 20–21, 41–42, 85, 87, 99, 106
Libyan relations, 100–103, 107, 109–110
Middle East relations, 41, 44, 48–49, 53, 71–72, 75–76, 78, 105, 111–112, 115, 118–119
Soviet relations, 49, 122
University of Havana, 82
University of Mosul, 82
Uruguay, 9
U.S.S.R. *See* Union of Soviet Socialist Republics

Valenta, Jiri, 18
Venezuela, 9, 11, 14, 104, 126

Western Europe, 119

YAR. *See* Yemen Arab Republic
Yemen Arab Republic (YAR), 4, 37, 68–69, 90, 93–94, 118–119
Yemeni Peoples' Defense Committees, 68
Yom Kippur War (1973), 40, 45, 55
Yugoslavia, 53, 83

Zambia, 87
Zionism, 28, 41, 48
opposition, 40, 53–54, 68, 73–76, 91, 104–105, 107, 109
U.N. resolutions, 88, 91